To Brian and Leah Foutz

I am both Honored and Deeply Blessed to be asked to read "Steps of Faith" Book Two by Brian and Leah Foutz.

I read their first Book "From Misery to Ministry" and found it to be one of the most inspiring Books I have ever read.

Steps of Faith is greatly uplifting with Joy and their inner-weaving of their first Book with their new Book is extraordinary and noteworthy!

It is evident that Brian and Leah walk closely with The Lord as shown in how God has "relocated" them many times for them to stay the true course and fulfill God's timely plan for of us. Romans 8:28 tells us "We know that all things work together for good to them that love God, to them who are called according to His purpose." To God be the Glory. I am blessed with a large Christian family, friends and involvement in Church worship activities. May God continue to Bless Brian and Leah on their journey for God.

A Friend in Christ,
MS in Texas

STEPS
of Faith

Blessings,
Leah

Brian

STEPS of Faith

BRIAN & LEAH FOUTZ

TATE PUBLISHING
AND ENTERPRISES, LLC

Scripture quotations marked (AMP) are taken from the *Amplified Bible*, Copyright © 1954, 1958, 1962, 1964, 1965, 1987 by The Lockman Foundation. Used by permission.

Scripture quotations marked (ESV) are from *The Holy Bible, English Standard Version*®, copyright © 2001 by Crossway Bibles, a publishing ministry of Good News Publishers. Used by permission. All rights reserved.

Scripture quotations marked (GNT) are from the *Good News Translation in Today's English Version*- Second Edition Copyright © 1992 by American Bible Society. Used by Permission.

Scripture quotations marked (KJV) are taken from the *Holy Bible, King James Version*, Cambridge, 1769. Used by permission. All rights reserved.

Scripture quotations marked (NASB) are taken from the *New American Standard Bible*®, Copyright © 1960, 1962, 1963, 1968, 1971, 1972, 1973, 1975, 1977, 1995 by The Lockman Foundation. Used by permission.

Scripture quotations marked (NIV) are taken from the *Holy Bible, New International Version*®, NIV®. Copyright © 1973, 1978, 1984 by Biblica, Inc.™ Used by permission of Zondervan. All rights reserved worldwide. www.zondervan.com

Scripture quotations marked (NKJV) are taken from the *New King James Version*. Copyright © 1982 by Thomas Nelson, Inc. Used by permission. All rights reserved.

Scripture quotations marked (NLT) are taken from the *Holy Bible, New Living Translation*, copyright © 1996. Used by permission of Tyndale House Publishers, Inc., Wheaton, Illinois 60189. All rights reserved.

Scripture quotations marked (TLB) are taken from *The Living Bible* / Kenneth N. Taylor: Tyndale House, © Copyright 1997, 1971 by Tyndale House Publishers, Inc. Used by permission. All rights reserved.

Scripture quotations marked (MSG) are taken from *The Message*. Copyright © 1993, 1994, 1995, 1996, 2000, 2001, 2002. Used by permission of NavPress Publishing Group.

Scripture quotations marked (WE) are taken from *THE JESUS BOOK–The Bible in Worldwide English*. Copyright SOON Educational Publications, Derby DE65 6BN, UK. Used by permission.

This book is designed to provide accurate and authoritative information with regard to the subject matter covered. This information is given with the understanding that neither the author nor Tate Publishing, LLC is engaged in rendering legal, professional advice. Since the details of your situation are fact dependent, you should additionally seek the services of a competent professional.

The opinions expressed by the author are not necessarily those of Tate Publishing, LLC.

Published by Tate Publishing & Enterprises, LLC
127 E. Trade Center Terrace | Mustang, Oklahoma 73064 USA
1.888.361.9473 | www.tatepublishing.com

Tate Publishing is committed to excellence in the publishing industry. The company reflects the philosophy established by the founders, based on Psalm 68:11,
"The Lord gave the word and great was the company of those who published it."

Book design copyright © 2016 by Tate Publishing, LLC. All rights reserved.
Cover design by Albert Ceasar Compay
Interior design by Gram Telen

Published in the United States of America

ISBN: 978-1-68319-660-0
1. Religion / Christian Ministry / General
2. Religion / Christian Life / General
16.06.03

This book was an inspiration by God, who, through many divine encounters gave us the wonderful stories to share with you our readers. It was through these divine encounters that we learned to take those steps of faith and to be led by The Holy Spirit.

If you want to live a joyful life, seek the Lord with all your heart. And when you do, He will give you the desires of your heart.

Let Him direct your steps and you will find an exciting journey waiting for you!

We hope and pray that this book will encourage you and your loved ones. Remember, in your travels, it is not about the distance, but the journey!

—Brian and Leah Foutz

Acknowledgements

Brian and I want to thank our Lord and Savior Jesus Christ for His Presence in our lives; for His Love and Guidance.

A special thank-you to all of those who the Lord used in arranging these divine encounters which took place in our lives.

We always find it *amazing* when the Lord uses His people for His purpose and for His Kingdom.

We also wish to thank our dear friend Suzanne Graham, who has graciously helped us to edit this—our second book! Suzanne, your help is, as always, appreciated and special to us! When we began talking about a second book there was never a moment of hesitation when thinking of someone to proofread and help us with any changes! Thank you again for your friendship and your assistance—once again! You *ROCK*, girl!

Contents

Foreword

I met Leah in Sunday school when we were both eight years old. We became lifelong friends. When we were in high school she saved my life—literally. I could have drowned in Galveston Bay. After college, God again planted us in the same city, and in the same church. I remember when she introduced me to Brian and instantly knew God had brought them together. They were a perfect match. I remember when Victoria was born, and I remember her coming to my house to visit. She was incredibly curious and creative. I always thought of her as a little elf or a sprite.

I remember when Brian called to tell me that Victoria had been murdered. My heart broke. I began to pray that God would Romans 8:28[1] what appeared to be a hopeless and tragic situation. It has been joy beyond measure to see how God has indeed given Leah and Brian a ministry that could have been born only out of incredible suffering and could only have been given to two people totally committed to Him.

I was one of the proofers for their first book, *From Misery to Ministry*. I read the last chapters from a hotel

---

1   "We know that all things work together for good to those who love God, to those who are the called according to His purpose."

room the night before my mother's funeral. It was as if God stepped in and spoke to me about grief and hope through their words.

What a privilege to be involved in editing the chapters for their new book, *Steps of Faith*. This is a book about Brian and Leah's journey as God has showed them how to walk step by step in faith. Each chapter is a vignette, a little glimpse into their lives at moments when God taught them life changing lessons. Some chapters are very happy; some are a little sad. Some will make you laugh; others will bring a tear to your eye.

Though the book is about events in Leah and Brian's lives, they will point you to take steps of faith in your own life. They will inspire you to look for God's hand in surprising places and unexpected moments in your day.

Enjoy reading!

—Susanne Graham
New Braunfels, Texas
PracticalPhoto-Publishing.com

The Journey Begins

Brian

> Then the LORD replied: "Write down the revelation
> and make it plain on tablets so that a herald may run
> with it. For the revelation awaits an appointed time;
> it speaks of the end and will not prove false. Though
> it linger, wait for it; it will certainly come and will
> not delay."
>
> —Habakkuk 2:2 (NIV)

It was the middle of the night and there I was, lying comfortably in our nice king-size bed.

I was in a deep sleep and having an incredible dream.

Suddenly, a voice entered right in the middle of my dream and I heard this: "I want you to write a book. You shall title this book *From Misery to Ministry: A Walk of Faith*." "Okay," I said, "yeah, that's cool. I will do that in the morning."

Like most people, it was back to la-la land.

I resumed my dream. Then, just like somebody knocking at your door, the voice returned. "Get up now and write this down."

I was thinking at this point, *Yeah, yeah, just five more minutes!*

The voice returned again. "*No!* I said get up now! Go to the computer and write this down now!"

Okay, okay, I'm up! I am moving, here I go, and with that I crawled out of bed.

My bride, Leah, who was also in a deep sleep, awoke and said to me, "Are you okay? What is it?"

"I am fine! Go back to sleep!" I bark. I know…it's rough getting up in the middle of the night (no pun intended).

At this point, I found myself thinking, *What on earth am I doing?* Was this a voice from God or was it the pizza I ate earlier tonight?

So I got up and haphazardly walked down the hall, glad there were two walls on both sides of me or I probably would have fallen down.

When I walked into my office, I closed the door, turned on the light, and then turned on the computer screen.

The computer is running all of the time, so while I waited for the program to open, I looked around, wondering if anyone else was up, you know…like my wife. Nope, just me!

I noticed the date and time down in the lower corner of the computer screen.

November 15, 2007. 1:30 a.m. Man! This is too early!

I then opened up my "ideas folder" on my Windows writing program and just started typing. As I began to type, the following words jumped onto the screen:

"The Lord spoke to me this morning, through a vision, on writing a book. Like an audible voice He said, the name of the book is to be "From Misery to Ministry—A Walk of Faith."

Wow! I thought. *What a cool name.* As I started to type some more, He revealed to me that I was to write out the chapters first, then write the book. There was to be an introduction or foreword and an invitation at the end of the book. Then He gave the following chapters to write.

"The first chapter was to be written myself, and I was to share about the day Victoria went home to be with the Lord." As I was sitting there, tears were coming down my face, and I was not even thinking, all I was doing was typing. Then words just began to appear in my mind, and I began typing.

The words were still coming into my tired and sleepy brain:

"Begin the story with the day that the two sheriffs arrived at the house—then backtrack to where we were two weeks before—then the year and a half before Victoria's death."

I remember typing as fast as I could for that early in the morning. When I type, I sometimes use the Christopher Columbus Method for typing…you know…. Search—Find—Land!

Then, the next phrase appeared in my mind: "The next chapter was to be Leah's story of Thursday, March 18. Write the next chapter on our life before her death."

I seemed to pause for a moment, and then resumed typing, "Our life before the tragedy. Talk about our family life—Victoria's rebellion, our marriage, life struggles, and the days before the loss."

At this point, I was just a blubbering and broken man, not knowing what to do next. I was awestruck. I found myself talking out loud in the room. No one else was there but me.

"I cannot write a book. I do not know how. I do not have the skills and gifts that it takes to do something like this."

When I tell people about that night, this was the moment where I looked up at God and said in that Randy Quaid actor's voice, "Are you sure?"

I asked God out loud, "Are you sure you want me to write this?"

I remember thinking, *I wonder if I should tell Leah about this dream? Oh wait, let me ask her now!*

No! I did not go and wake her up—I let her sleep. You know what they say: "A happy wife is a happy life!"

Over the next few months I would, from time to time, go and look at the "book idea" file folder. Then out of nowhere, another thought would come to my mind and I would write down that thought for another chapter in the book.

I am a firm believer that these creative and good thoughts come from our creator. And that He, our Lord, gives us these promptings.

> Every good thing given and perfect gift is from above, coming down from the Father of lights, with whom there is no variation or shifting shadow. (James 1:17, NASB)

There never really seemed to be a sense of urgency on the surface, but I know there was one just below the surface. It must have been three or four months after this dream that I mentioned to the members in our ministry band about my dream and vision for writing a book. Several of them related that I should go ahead and write it. But the clouds of doubt popped back in my head, and I just left the idea alone.

Over the next year I would open up the file, more by accident than anything else. I would see what was jotted down, then an idea or two would come into my head and I would write these ideas down, save the file and would say, "I need to come back and look at this later."

Here is something to ponder:

You know we all hear the words from our pastors, teachers, and friends about God's will and His timing. We nod our heads and go through the motions of agreeing with them, but do we really spend time in prayer and ask for His will?

This proved to be just one of the many future opportunities of seeing God at work and how He works to bring things about in His time. This is just another reminder of the process in taking a step of faith.

In January 2008 I began to take a series of seminary classes offered by Grace Fellowship United Methodist Church in Katy, Texas.

Our instructor, Paul Helbig, gave us our first assignment: we were to read James 1:2–4 and write out twenty-five to thirty observations on these verses. Basically, we were to look up every word in the passage and write what it means and how it is used in the verses. Wow! This was pretty intense to say the least.

The class met the following week. We spent a great deal of time on this assignment, and we literally ran out of time, so it was decided to come back the following week to finish up.

When the class returned the following week, the teacher asked if anyone had anything special to say about these verses and how they may have impacted their life. I slowly lifted my hand and was called on next.

I shared how these verses were very important to both my wife and me and how these verses brought us hope for the future.

I began to share with the class that fateful Thursday morning of March 18, 2004. I shared that our daughter Victoria was supposed to be at a friend's home in Katy on Wednesday, the night before.

We thought she was okay and would be home the next day. The next morning, two detectives arrived at my home and had to inform me that our daughter's body had been found that morning with a gunshot wound to the head. I then went on to share about our shock, horror, grief, and how we wondered what to do next.

Then I told them how God showed up, answering our prayers, and giving us that "perfect peace" to walk through this storm of life.

I then read James 1:2–4 (NASB) for the class:

> Consider it all joy, my brethren, when you encounter various trials, knowing that the testing of your faith produces endurance. And let endurance have its perfect result, so that you may be perfect and complete, lacking in nothing.

I then shared "that this death of our only child was indeed a trial. A trial both Leah and I never wanted and one that we could not handle. This was a testing of our faith, and this kind of faith does produce endurance. As we experienced that testing, we were both being made perfect and whole in Him, lacking nothing."

There was silence throughout the room. Tears and sniffling were everywhere. When I finished, there was an amazing outpouring of the Holy Spirit, and many were comforted by the story. Many came up to me later and shared that they had no idea what had happened in our lives. But, to hear the story, to see the look of peace on my face, and to hear God's love and compassion in the story gave them hope.

So, how does this fit into God's timing in the big picture?

A lady sitting next to me named Janice would become a good class friend over the next couple of years. One day in February 2009, I was showing Janice a picture of our girl, Victoria. Janice shared that after I spoke to the class, she had gone home and had done an internet search on our daughter and learned more about the murder, capture, and trial.

She then looked at me and said, "Brian, have you ever thought about writing a book on your journey?" I looked up at her and gave her this really big grin.

"Funny you should ask that, I had this dream about eighteen months ago about writing a book. God gave me this really neat title for a book called *From Misery to Ministry: A Walk of Faith*. You know, I need to find someone to help us with editing and putting a book together. It seems like all of the good writers do this. Do you know anyone who does this?"

She looked intensely back at me. "Yes, I do know someone who does this."

With some excitement, I said, "Well, could you send me their name and phone number? I would like to call them."

To this Janice replied, "Yes I can, in fact *I* do editing and help others with their books." Praise God! Was this cool or what!

When I got home I shared with Leah about my conversation with Janice, and this, as they would say, was the beginning of a new season in writing a book. Janice became a close friend and ally in the writing and editing of our book.

Isn't it interesting how God uses His timing to align people and things up for Him, and His will?

Dr. Myles Munroe stated in his book *The Principles and Power of Vision* that when we get a vision from God, we are not prepared for this vision. He will give us the vision long before He gives us the provision, because God has to prepare us first.

Then He begins to properly align everything else so that when it is time—everything we need will be there waiting for us.

These are just some of the ways that we learn to take those first steps of faith.

Joy in Healing

Leah

> The Lord is my strength and my shield; my heart
> trusts in him, and he helps me. My heart leaps for
> joy, and with my song I praise him.
>
> —Psalms 28:7 (NIV)

I am a seeker. Whatever I am doing, I have learned to seek God's hand in everything. This is not easy for me, since I am pretty stubborn and like to have my own way all the time!

God has taken the natural desire of my heart (to be a seeker) and allowed me to incorporate my curiosity into daily life.

Life is a great gift! No matter whether it is "good" or "bad," it is incredible just to live it. When we allow God to structure our days however, our lives become truly amazing! God will take something that seems so very insignificant and make it new and wonderful. He's like that. God wants us to enjoy our lives here on this earth while doing things to make a difference for Him.

One of the lessons I have learned from this life on earth is that everything we go through counts as a "life lesson," and we learn from each and every one of these lessons. When we allow *God* to guide us through these lessons however, we will learn greater things which will in turn help us to be more like our Savior Jesus Christ, who went around doing His Father's will.

That is the highest calling for a human being to have, to learn, and to live! At this time in my life here on earth, the most prominent lesson I am learning is to have *pure joy* in every area of my life.

Now, you may be thinking that there are some things in this life that are definitely *not* an opportunity to be joyful, and you are correct.

However, in the Bible it tells us to be joyful at *all* times, no matter what we are going through.

In the book of James we learn to count everything that we go through as joy.

> Consider it pure joy, my brothers, whenever you face trials of many kinds, because you know that the testing of your faith develops perseverance. Perseverance must finish its work so that you may be mature and complete, not lacking anything. (James 2:2–4, NIV)

There are many opportunities for us to be joyful in life, even when it seems as if nothing is good or right. For example, many of us have pets in our homes. These animals give us their complete devotion (probably because we feed them!) and we love them very much.

However, because of the ways of life and longevity, it is fairly certain that we will outlive our precious pets. When a pet dies, we go through a time of mourning, weeping, and missing that special animal. I have lost many pets over the years; some to old age, but others due to illness or accidental death. Believe me: no matter how your pet died you will be sad, sometimes to the point of devastation.

In our minds, we tend to rerun everything that we did to keep them from dying, fearing that there was some way we could have averted this loss, but that is a trap for us!

We usually cannot stop the order of life and death for our pets. We mourn their death for a time, and then an amazing thing begins to happen! We begin to remember the joy that we had with these animals, how they acted as babies, growing up and playing with us.

We still feel the sense of loss. However, we begin to heal, and remember mostly the good times they brought to us. This is growth into God's joy!

There are many, many types of trials, many times of being hurt in our lives. There are situations that we live through that make no sense to us, but that can be very hurtful for a long time if we let them.

For example, take a job that may have ended badly. When we start a new job we are excited. We are hoping to contribute something that the company needs. Our expectations are high at the onset.

Sometimes, however, something changes along the way. We begin to experience some degree of dissatisfaction with the position itself or with people that we interact with on a regular basis. If we let these situations continue, we can develop resentments and/or a poor attitude. That can be trouble. Not only will these attitudes affect the job performance we give, it will also affect relationships within our work environment.

These things can lead to even more resentment, and may even lead to you being let go from the job, or you leave on your own. We need to look at our own behaviors and see whether or not the results were because of our actions. Either way, we must learn to look forward, not backward, in our lives.

I once had a position with a company that was extremely difficult for me. There was a lot of work to be done, and some of those in our department did not get along very well, especially during times of tight deadlines. This situation caused several of us to develop poor attitudes, and eventually our work production began to suffer. One of the results of this situation was that several of our group resigned or were laid off. I was one of them. "Company downsizing" was the reason given when I was laid off. That was a prime example of something that I could have developed resentment over.

I had been having a difficult time with one of my coworkers. We just did not see eye to eye, and I suspected that she was badmouthing me to our supervisors. I knew that God would want me to be loving and kind no matter what this person did or said, so I began to pray for salvation and for peace.

You might think that God ignored me by letting things get to the point of my being laid off. However, you would be incorrect.

God has a plan for each of us. However, He also has a plan for our rescue if necessary! I believe that God took me out of an uncomfortable situation so that He could use me elsewhere. I realized that He had intervened in that way. I had been faithful to pray for this person all along, no matter what, and God knew that my heart was true. He rescued me! I have been able to forgive the negative things that went on at that job, and He has blessed me even more because I still remember to pray for the other person!

In other words, situations like mine don't have to be awful; we have a God who loves us and will teach us His ways in *any* situation we are put into, even when that situation is very difficult.

> No temptation has overtaken you except what is common to mankind. And God is faithful; he will not let you be tempted beyond what you can bear. But when you are tempted, he will also provide a way out so that you can endure it. (1 Cor. 10:13, NIV)

See what I mean?

God is very actively involved with our lives when we are His children! He sees everything, and trusts us to act in the way that Jesus would act. When we do, He rewards us by helping us to *endure* the situation or rescuing us *from* the situation! Praise Him!

Remembering previous examples of His care for us and His provisions during times of pain and suffering are good for us. God will never give us more than we can handle—that is, more than *He* and we can handle together. Brian and I found that out in 2004 in a very real way. Let me tell you about it.

We are parents of a beautiful and intelligent young woman, Victoria. She was the apple of our eyes, and we loved her as God's gift to us. However, all things did not go quite as we had planned. In March of 2004, just after her eighteenth birthday, Victoria was murdered by three young men who had offered her a ride. They were casual friends of hers, and she trusted them to take her home as she had asked them to. Her body was found the next morning in a field with a gunshot wound to the face. Of course, Brian and I were devastated!

When you hear tragic news like that, the first thing you will feel is shock. Mind-numbing shock. *How could this happen?* That was what went through my mind as I unsuccessfully attempted to understand, comprehend, and accept what I had just been told.

After the initial shock, I was able to begin asking God why this had happened. It was a difficult conversation, especially since Victoria was our only child. God's response was gentle, loving, and kind. My heart was broken, my faith was shaken, and I did not know how to feel!

However, my God knew what I was going through, and within forty-eight hours of her death, His peace and love covered both Brian and me like a soft fluffy blanket. We experienced a time of hope and love from God that overcame the pain of our loss. We had the confidence that Victoria was with Him in heaven, and even though our earthly hearts had been broken, we knew that we would see her again in heaven.

Once again, God had taken something awful, something devastating, and turned it into a time of praising Him. Remember that verse in James? We have been able to count even our daughter's murder as an occasion for joy, and we love Him for His faithfulness.

One thing I have learned over the years is this quote by Robert Schuller: "Joy is not the absence of sorrow; it is the presence of God."

My God is not an "old man with a beard," sitting up in heaven tossing down fiery darts upon me and my life; He is my heavenly "Daddy," and He loves me! The devil is the one who hates me and wants me to hate God. I do not live for the devil; I live for Christ!

> And having shod your feet with the preparation of the gospel of peace; in addition to all, taking up the shield of faith with which you will be able to extinguish all the flaming arrows of the evil one. (Eph. 6:15–16, NASB)

A New Drive and a New Journey

Brian

> A man's mind plans his way, but the Lord directs his steps and makes them sure.
>
> —Proverbs 16:9 (AMP)

One of the great pleasures of going for a drive is learning to find an alternate route—you know, "the back roads."

This gets you off the main highway and away from the tension and anxiety of being on a major road. At times it seems that everyone around you is pushing you from behind and wanting you to go faster, but…stay out of *their* way! I have shared with many people over the years that when traveling, it is not about the distance but about the journey.

When you look at a trip as a journey, you learn to relax more, enjoy the scenery, and spend quality time with your spouse, friend, or loved one as you drive. It is also a great way to just spend time with God.

One of our journeys happened on a particular Sunday in November of 2008. Our ministry band, The Daystar Project, had the opportunity of leading the service at Christian Faith Church in Bellville, Texas. Back in 1999, Leah and I had both been to the church together when we did a New Year's Eve service.

That had been when everyone was planning for the infamous Y2K and the possible havoc that it might cause. *Not!* During the years that followed, I had been blessed with the opportunity to play keyboards at the church on several occasions with my friend Don, as well as some other events with the band.

That Sunday in November 2008 was a special occasion for me because on this day, I would be able to share the sermon message. During the past year, the Lord had begun to use me in a new way—to bring a message of hope, healing, and encouragement to others. This was possible through His Word in the scriptures and through our story of restoration and preparation for ministry.

The message that day was about God's promise to His people after bringing them out of the land of Egypt from captivity and taking them to the Promised Land. God told them that in order to possess the land they would have to fight the Hittites, Girgashites, Amorites, Canaanites, Perizzites, Hivites, and Jebusites. *Yikes!*

My sermon was on "The Battle of the -Ites." The overall message was this: In life, God will give you a vision. With that vision, He will give you a promise, a plan, and a process, just as He did for His chosen people.

But somewhere along the line, the enemy will come along and speak doubt into your life, just as the spies who went into the Promised Land came back said, "There are giants in them thar hills!"

Ten of the twelve spies said this was *way too much to do* and spoke *doubt* into the leaders of the people. This doubt became their obstacle from moving forward with God's plan.

So, because of their lack of faith, they got to do "Ground Hog Day" for the next forty years until they got it right. After forty years when that generation of doubters had died off, God finally let them cross the River Jordan and go into the Promised Land.

This was an incredible message, not only for those who attended that day, but it would serve as a wakeup call for Leah and me as well. This call reminded us of what the Lord was about to do in our lives.

In the following months, Leah and I would drive back to this church every Sunday to "visit" and hear a message on blessing and favour. Our plan was to just go and hear the sermon series and nothing more. No agenda. Ha!

During this time, one of my prayers had been asking God to give Leah a place of happiness and rest to spend time with Him in the Word on Sunday. We had been happy at our church but felt a tugging on our hearts, we wanted more, but I could not tell what this tugging was all about.

In our prayer time, we felt that we had not been given permission to leave our church in Katy yet, and to be honest with you, we were really *not* looking for another church at the time.

> And without faith it is impossible to please Him, for he who comes to God must believe that He is and that He is a rewarder of those who seek Him. (Heb. 11:6, NASB)

Our steps of faith journey continued in January when Christian Faith Church was hosting the annual AEGA (the Association of Evangelical Gospel Assemblies) Conference. Leah and I had never attended this type of conference before and wanted to go. This was still very new to us.

Our usual Sunday drive to Bellville would take us from Katy, down some back roads, through Pattison, Texas, turn left, go across the Brazos River near a town called Burleigh, and on into Bellville. It is a beautiful scenic drive with very little traffic. This is a perfect drive for anyone who would like to go for a drive in the country and view the scenery. Remember, it is not about the distance but the journey!

This particular Sunday, God would begin to bring change into our lives. This was a divine intersection; a type of encounter that would forever change who we are, and a change of where God was about to lead us.

Leah and I were enjoying the beautiful clear morning while I drove on the quiet little road to church. As I made our left turn from Pattison onto Highway 529, I looked over at my beautiful bride. To my surprise she had this bright red nose and tears running down her face.

"Hey, are you okay?" I asked. Crying, with a happy voice she replied, "Yes, I just *love* this drive." (Sniff, sniff)

Wow! I thought to myself. I cannot remember ever seeing her like this before. She is so happy and crying just about being on a drive on this morning!

A little further down the road, we crossed over the bridge on the Brazos River. As we passed, I could hear her crying, looked over at her, and asked her another question. "Sweetie, what's the matter? Are you okay?"

Crying happily, she again replied, "I just love the people at our church!" Wow! She has never been this emotional about a church before. She has liked most of the churches that we ever visited and joined, but nothing like this. She never cried and was happy about going to a church at the same time. The drive, the people, the love that we felt at this church would forever change our lives and direction.

They say that God will speak to us through His Word, through His Spirit, through circumstances, our surroundings, through others, and our prayers.

A divine encounter was about to take place, and Leah was not prepared for what came next.

During the month of January, Leah had been laid off from a company that she had been with for three and half years. It had been a good company, and one that was fun to work for.

But "change happens." The company was bought by another company, and with mergers come downsizing, which lead to layoffs. Nothing personal, "it's not you" employers would say…just that suddenly there are more people than positions available.

For Leah, the stress and the layoff were very hard and personal. She was not sure what she was going to do. She was concerned because several other companies in her field were also laying people off and no one was hiring. She was very upset about this and had been crying out to God for help.

What was she going to do for work? What about the loss of income to the family? How was she going to be able to help us? All good questions, as my friend Stephen Coffee would say.

Okay, here comes the divine encounter. God is so cool!

While we were at church in Bellville, people were coming by to say hello. You know, the typical greeting one gets in the church. "Good morning," "it is nice to see you," "thank you for coming this morning," "have good day." Blah, blah, blah.

Anyway, this nice man—his name was Ray—came by the pew where Leah was sitting, greeted her, and then walked away. A footnote here: neither Leah nor I had ever met this man until this day.

I was standing on the outside of the aisle when he walked passed after greeting her. Then suddenly…he turned around and went back to where Leah was sitting.

He told her, "The Lord just gave me a Word for you. He told me to tell you that you do not have to worry about your job—that God will provide for you and everything that you need."

Leah sat there stunned, I mean stunned! And she just started crying and weeping. For this was the first time that someone had ever given her a Word from the Lord. She was raised as a "good Baptist girl," and yes, this—this was an answer to her prayer! Again, she just sat there and cried and cried. Yes—this was a happy cry.

Leah would later be given a small separation package from work, with extended unemployment benefits and a chance to keep her health insurance for almost two years. This would allow Leah to stay at home, help coauthor our book and allow us to begin our new encouragement ministry.

So, a new step of faith took place. And this step would become part of the next new drive and another new journey. Indeed, as each day goes by, we are constantly reminded of His faithfulness and His answers to prayers.

> See, I am doing a new thing! Now it springs up; do you not perceive it? I am making a way in the wilderness and streams in the wasteland. (Is. 43:19, NIV)

Steps of Faith: The Basics

Brian

> Now go, write it on a tablet before them, and inscribe
> it on a scroll, that it may serve in the time to come as
> a witness forever.
>
> —Isaiah 30:8 (NASB)

I am often asked, "Brian, you talk about being led by the Spirit and learning to walk by faith. What does this look like? Are there really steps that one has to learn to walk by faith?"

As we have shared with many of our friends, partners, and prayer warriors: you have to have faith to make it in this world. And if you really want to make an impact in your life and in the lives of those around you, then you have to learn to take steps each day in your faith.

Some of these will be baby steps at first. But just like a baby, as you grow in your faith, you learn to take longer and bigger steps and let the Lord guide you in the pathway of life.

After the loss of Victoria, Leah and I went through a period of restoration of our marriage and through a grieving period of loss. Then the Lord began our next journey of preparation. At first we thought this preparation was only a change from a husband and wife with a child to just a married couple coping with a childless family.

But the Lord had other plans. This type of preparation would be one of getting the two of us ready for ministry. We were already doing music ministry with our band but, really, a ministry?

For me, I never thought of myself being a minister or helping others, because I thought I was doing that type of ministry through music.

I remember someone once said that out of your greatest misery, God would birth your greatest ministry.

For us, this would become our banner for serving Him and doing work for His Kingdom.

For it is all about doing Kingdom work and using Kingdom Principles.

> Our first instruction from Jesus is to seek. This means to pursue, study, explore, understand, learn, and consider. Seekers must have a desire to know, and possess a passion for the object of their search. To seek means to give diligent dedication to and to preoccupy one's self with that which one is seeking. The Kingdom must be pursued, studied, understood, and learned. (Dr. Myles Munroe, *Kingdom Principles*, 39)

> But seek first His kingdom and his righteousness, and all these things will be given to you as well. (Matt. 6:33, NIV)

Leah and I would begin to see these steps of faith take hold in our life as we began moving closer into full time ministry.

You see there is no blueprint, or a piece of paper that states, "Go do this and that, and this is how you will do it." It is something that takes time, it takes prayer and it takes faith.

> Now faith is the substance of things hoped for, the evidence of things not seen. (Heb. 11:1, KJV)

It has been amazing to see how the Lord has moved us, not only in location and residence, but also by moving us closer to Him on our spiritual journey.

Leah and I wanted to share this special chapter with you on how God worked in our lives. May you find comfort, strength, and perseverance. May you may be blessed in your own spiritual journey!

After moving to the rolling hills of New Ulm, Texas, Leah and I began to sense a new and different direction to our lives. It would change how we thought, how we planned our life, and it would take us on a new and uncharted journey.

There is an old saying in life: "If you want to make God laugh, just tell him your plans!"

You can have well thought out plans, charts, and figures, but until you really know your purpose here on earth and what God has made you to do, you will never be truly happy and you will never be fulfilled. No brag, just fact.

During our morning home Bible study in 2012, Leah and I had been really digging deep into God's Word. We were looking for "more of Him" and what He would have us to do. One of our studies was by Chuck Pierce called *50 Days to Staking Your Claim for Your Future and Opening Supply Lines*.

It was a powerful study. In fact, this was our second time to go through the daily study, and we were amazed by some of the things we missed on the first go round. Hey, nobody is perfect!

Over the next couple of years, we learned some really important lessons in taking steps of faith. Leah and I want to share some of those basic steps with you and some of our true-life experiences that came with these divine encounters and steps.

With that, here are some helpful ideas in learning to understand the basics in steps of faith:

1. **Learn to Praise**

    We have to learn that there is power in praise. Learn to praise Him each and every day.

    Yes, praise Him for everything and for all things. Every morning when we first open our eyes, we should praise Him for being on the top side of the grass. Why? Because we are alive! Praise Him for our health. Yes, praise Him for our health. It does not matter if our health is perfect or poor, for through Him all things are made, and He can heal our broken bodies. Praise Him for our position and situation and our station in life. Why? Because God can use us regardless of where we live and work.

From his book *Power in Praise*, Merlin R. Carothers shared this:

> Always be joyful. Always keep on praying. No matter what happens, always be thankful, for this is God's will for you who belong to Christ Jesus.
>
> Rejoice always; pray without ceasing; in everything give thanks; for this is God's will for you in Christ Jesus. (1 Thess. 5:16–18, NASB).

Leah and I have learned to praise Him, even during our time of grief after losing Victoria. We gave Him thanks for the supernatural peace that He gave to us when He answered our prayers!

2. **Learn to Yield**

Wow! Learn to yield. So what does that really mean? Over in the Webster's Dictionary, they define yield like this:

a. To give up, as in defeat; surrender or submit.

b. To give way to pressure or force.

c. To give way to argument, persuasion, influence, or entreaty.

d. To give up one's place, as to one that is superior.

Now this same word in Hebrew is *Nathan*, which means "to give, bestow, grant, permit, ascribe, employ, devote, consecrate, dedicate, pay wages, sell, exchange, lend, commit, entrust, or give over."

Basically when we yield, we give up. That means give up everything.

Think of it this way. When you were a child, for whatever reason you found yourself in a fight that you were losing. The other child was on top of you and had you pinned down. They would say, "Yield! Do you yield?" It was at that point you yielded or gave up. They won and let you go.

Now when we yield in warfare, it means that we are laying down *all* of our arms, shield and armor, and the fighting stops. There is no more aggression and we yield to the conquering forces or king. We find ourselves submitting to them and taking an oath of allegiance. When that happens, we are now under their authority.

When we yield to Jesus, we are to submit to His authority. We now yield to the King, for He is the King of Kings and Lord of Lords!

We have to learn to yield in all things. In order to have His power in healing, prophecy, and learning the mysteries of life; we have to yield to Him. We do this so that we can be used by Him, for Him, and to help others.

> Yield now and be at peace with Him; Thereby good will come to you. (Job 22:21, NASB)

Smith Wigglesworth shared this about learning to yield to Him who made us:

> "Behold, now is the day of decision. Yield now while the moment of pressure by the presence of God comes. Yield now and make your consecration to God."

This quote is one of my all time favorite quotes from Smith Wigglesworth: "What would you have me do?" That is just awesome!

3. **Learn to Encourage**

Yes, learn to encourage everyone that we meet. We live in a hurting world. The enemy loves to roam this earth wanting to lie, cheat, deceive, hurt, and even kill the people of this world.

> Be of sober spirit, be on the alert. Your adversary, the devil, prowls around like a roaring lion, seeking someone to devour. (1 Pet. 5:8, NASB)

We are constantly bombarded on a daily basis with negative thoughts, innuendoes, sexual deviance, perversion, and the tearing down of one's honesty, makeup, and convictions. We are told to live life to the fullest with disregard for others and their feelings. People say to do it because we deserve to have anything and everything. But when we do this, we fall for the lie—the lie that Satan uses to discourage God's people.

People need to feel that they have worth; that they have value and meaning in this world.

We all struggle daily with something. It can be our finances, our health, our spouses and children, our family, our careers and work, or our possessions. We find ourselves asking, is the car working properly? What about the lawn mower, the bicycle, the boat, our guns, fishing equipment, camera, iPhone, or computer?

Oh my, the computer! The computer has to be updated constantly! There are glitches and hitches in programs. Files are being updated and deleted. New downloads must be approved. Spyware, viruses, and worms try to embed themselves into the fabric of everything we store. And of course…the printer! We need more ink, more paper, more toner. I have to print those new pictures out. I need more memory to do it faster…and on and on and on and on!

We have so much to worry about, and we are always asking something or someone for help. But where is the encouragement to keep going? Who is there to tell you that you are doing okay? And that, with help, things will be okay? Instruction manuals and online videos are okay. They can assist you with your problems or challenges. But where is the "personal" touch? Where is the help that you really need?

Our help comes from the Lord. He has called each and every one of us to help one another with His love and grace. We have to learn to reach out and touch someone, and to help them walk through the storms of life.

> Therefore encourage (admonish, exhort) one another and edify (strengthen and build up) one another, just as you are doing. (1 Thess. 5:11, AMP)

You see my friend, we are all human, and we need encouragement! We need to have that pat on the back or touch. We need someone saying, "Atta boy! Keep up the good work."

Possibly it is that little push that says, like in *The Little Engine That Could*, "I think I can, I think I can."

However, our response should be "I know I can, I know I can...I can do this...I can make it...with God's help I know I can...I know I can!"

We have all been called to encourage one another, but we have to learn an important fact: pray first. There is great danger of getting sucked into the drama of life. We do not help someone when we agree with the negativity of their life or join in their complaining. We also do not help someone if we make light of a problem that seems serious to them.

How about we stop and pray? Ask the Lord to show us how to focus on Him and what He would have us to do. We need to help others see His light in all things and find ways to look at the difficult things in life as challenges instead of problems.

4. **Learn to Love with God's love**

Wow! Now this is a tough one to learn to do. God told us to do everything in love, with His love. Why? Because Love is the greatest gift of all!

> And now these three remain: faith, hope and love. But the greatest of these is love. (1 Cor, 13:13, NIV)

Love conquers all. Not just some, but *all*. If it were not so, then why did Jesus give us these words to live by:

> Love is patient, love is kind and is not jealous; love does not brag and is not arrogant, does not act unbecomingly; it does not seek its own, is not provoked, does not take into account a wrong suffered, does not rejoice in unrighteousness, but rejoices with the truth; bears all things, believes all things, hopes all things, endures all things. (1 Cor.13: 4–8, NASB)

Yes, love conquers all. Jesus gave us these words, but they are not only words, they are a code to live by. Life will also give us a code to live by, but man's code can be broken by man. How's that, Brian?

I remember a line from the movie *Pirates of the Caribbean*. There was a young woman who had been taken captive by the pirates and wanted to "parley" or have a peace talk.

When the woman felt that she had bargained with the pirates and gotten what she thought she wanted, she suddenly found out that there was a new and different deal by the captain of the pirates. Different than what was agreed upon. She was shocked! She complained to the captain, "You have to agree to the terms that we discussed and you cannot change the deal! There is a *code* that all pirates live by, and you have to abide by that code!"

The captain's reply was classic! With a devious and twisted smile he said, "It's not really a code… they're more like guidelines!" I love this!

5. **Learn to be Open**

We have to learn to be open to the Lord's prompting. God will show us what we are to do. But we have to be prepared to go where He will send us.

So what does this look like? "Come on Brian, can't we just decide what to do and where to go?"

Sure you can, but do you want to be open to His will or yours? It's a choice. It's your choice.

So what does this word *open* mean?

It means to expose, free, or unfasten, and to be accessible, available, and willing! The Hebrew word for this is *gala*, and it means to uncover and to remove.

> Open my eyes, that I may behold wonderful things from your law. (Ps. 119:18, NASB)

Leah and I have had many divine intersections over the years. Divine encounters come when you meet someone and the Lord presents an opportunity for you to share His love and your testimony. This is a time when the Lord may use you to be a blessing for that a person, or they may be a blessing for you. Today we all need hope, and we all need encouragement. If you stay open, the Lord will give you an amazing encounter!

During some of our encounters, we suddenly found opportunities to share our story and our ministry. When this happens, we find that that person suddenly opens up and shares with us that they too lost a child or a loved one, or possibly it was one of their siblings or parent. And after they have shared, we find that some have not moved on from the loss, and others are in search of what to do next.

Leah and I continually ask the Lord to bring us to others who need help and to take us places to bring a powerful message of His love and restoration.

> Ask, and it will be given to you; seek, and you will find; knock, and it will be opened to you. For everyone who asks receives, and he who seeks finds, and to him who knocks it will be opened. (Matt. 7:7–8, NASB)

6. Learn to be Willing

We need to learn to be willing. The dictionary defines this as being prepared and being ready to do something gladly and eagerly and being cheerful about it.

> Pray for us: for we trust we have a good conscience, in all things willing to live honestly. (Heb. 13:18, KJV)

For us, this meant that we had to learn to change our thinking and our priorities. Over the years, when people called or came by the house, if we were busy we would put them off by rescheduling a time to meet and talk with them later. We found that people who called on us had a need. They needed someone to talk to, someone who would listen. The time was now, not later.

Our willingness to serve Him meant that we had to be willing to be used by Him when His opportunity arose. As we began to change our thinking, it was amazing to see how His hand was in everything and that we were just a small part of His overall plan.

Many times over the years I would leave the dinner table to take a call, or get up from a movie, or stop something else that I was doing. And when I did, I learned more about His will for our lives and for our ministry.

It is by no accident or coincidence that God brings you across someone's path. It has been well thought out in advance by our Creator, and all that you have to do is to be willing. When you are willing, awesome things happen right before your eyes!

> And you, my son Solomon, acknowledge the God of your father, and serve him with wholehearted devotion and with a willing mind, for the Lord searches every heart and understands every desire and every thought. If you seek Him, He will be found by you; but if you forsake Him, He will reject you forever. (1 Chron. 28:9, NIV)

7. Learn to be Obedient

Boy! This was a tough one for me to learn. The dictionary defines this word as "doing your duty and complying with the commands, orders, or instructions of one in authority." Ouch!

Now, *obedient* in Hebrew is the word *shamah*. It means to hear (perceive by ear); to listen and give heed; to consent and agree.

> Then he took the book of the covenant and read it in the hearing of the people; and they said, "All that the Lord has spoken we will do, and we will be obedient!" (Ex 24:7, NASB)

This was one of the hardest steps for me to learn and understand. You know, I'm a guy! Sometimes we have to do things our way first, and then give in and let God take over.

That means when everything seems to be out of whack and you are obedient, you stay the course, regardless of what is going on around you.

A lot of us do not want to give up control and we want to handle everything ourselves. Humanly speaking, there is nothing wrong with that. But if you want to be in God's will and do what He has called you to do, then you *have* to give up control.

My good friend Linda Moore sent me a note with regards to a decision that I was going to have to make. Her words cut straight through to the bone. She said, "Obedience demands sacrifice." That means that we let God be in charge, let Him be at the helm of the ship. When we do, He will direct our path through the storms and calm seas.

There is much more that we could share, but Leah and I felt that these seven steps would encourage you to take your own Steps of Faith.

We have found that when we are obedient, obedient to Him, everything else seems to fall right into place. The timing is perfect, the doors are opened and His provision comes through. By His grace, we are saved.

> Blessed is the man who perseveres under trial; for once he has been approved, he will receive the crown of life which the Lord has promised to those who love Him. (James 1:12, NASB)

Is This for Real?

Brian

> A man's mind plans his way, but the Lord directs his
> steps and makes them sure.
>
> —Proverbs 16:9 (AMP)

In our quest to seek the Lord further, Leah and I continued to read our Bible daily, digging and reaching deeper, but we also began to attend some teaching conferences on the Bible.

One of these led us to a conference at the House of Prayer in Conroe, Texas on October 29th, 2009. There we had the opportunity to meet and listen to some incredible teachers, Marty and Kathy Gabler.

It was a Saturday. I had previously gone to their monthly teaching in September, but Leah had decided to stay home. After returning from the Saturday teaching, I shared with Leah the notes that I had taken. She was excited with the information and looked at me and said, "Yeah…yeah, I know…I *should* have gone!"

So, this month she was going. When we got there, Leah was pleasantly surprised: no big fanfare, not a huge church with lots of people, just a small room that would hold about thirty people—but boy, could you feel the presence of God! It was awesome!

Marty began sharing about how people go about finding God. He said that today, people live contrary to the Word of God. Boy, that one caught us by surprise. I *thought* we were living in His will, but we soon found out what he meant.

He taught that in the Old Testament times people who wanted to find God "had to go and find the altar." Yes, the altar, and that when they found the altar, they would find Yahweh or God.

He continued by saying that when they found the altar and found God, the Lord would tell them where to place their tents, and then He would provide them with a well for their resources.

About now, you are probably thinking like I was thinking: *Whaaat?*

But wait…it gets better. Marty went on to say that in modern times, we live contrary to God's will. What *we* do is we first go and look for the job (i.e., the well) for our provisions. Then we start looking for a place to live (i.e., place to pitch our tent). Lastly, we begin to look for a church or place to worship.

Wow! This really resonated in our hearts and spirits, and we began to talk about this. When we are planning our lives, do we really include God in *all* of our plans, or just the ones where we feel that we need help? Deep down we believe we can take care of most of our plans ourselves.

> For My thoughts are not your thoughts, neither are
> your ways My ways, says the Lord. For as the heavens
> are higher than the earth, so are My ways higher than
> your ways and My thoughts than your thoughts. (Isa.
> 55:8–9, AMP)

The late Bob Jones had a great insight on how we should learn to live. Pointing to his stomach he said, "We need to learn to be led by the Spirit"—and then pointing to his head— "and not by the soul."

Leah and I discussed this in detail on our way home, and we shared about our lives and where God was leading us. We had been thinking about moving and been looking in the Austin County area. We were not ready to move or commit to anything at this time, but we did drive around the area and just dream.

The following morning, Sunday, Leah and I attended Christian Faith Church in Bellville, Texas. Preaching that morning was a small man from India who had a gift of prophesy and would share a "word" with different people.

At the end of the service, he looked out into the congregation and saw us sitting there. He motioned to us and said, "Could you both come up to the front, please?"

Leah and I walked up to the front of the church—we were just standing there—not really knowing what was going to take place. The preacher's name was Alfred, and he began to speak to the pastor and another man named James—praying for them, for the church, and families.

Then he turned to us. He began sharing some things with Leah about her life and how the Lord would use her to help both teens and other women in her walk and ministry.

He then turned to me and began to share that the Lord would use me in the area of a prophetic music ministry. I thought this was pretty interesting. I was not sure what this would look like. But, in time, the Lord would show me exactly what this would be. The Lord later would give me the music for my first keyboard album. I will share more on that music in another chapter.

Then something amazing happened. So much so that it caught Leah and me both by surprise.

We thought Alfred was finished with us, and we got ready to turn around and head back to our seats when he stopped us.

He said, "The Lord Yahweh has revealed to me that you two have been praying." Okay, I got this one. Yes, we had been praying—we are always praying. But we did have two specific prayers that we had shared with *no one*!

Then, these words came out of his mouth, "The Lord has shown me that you two have been praying and asking Him for a *time*. 'When is the *time* that you are going to use us and move us?' The time is *now*!"

Oh my! This was powerful. Leah grabbed my right arm with both of her hands. She almost fell down. She was crying and weeping—but these were tears of joy!

I stood there in awe—yes, in awe. I was thinking to myself, "There are only three people who know about this prayer. We have not told anyone about this. Two of us are standing here, and the other one is *invisible*!"

Wow! All that I can say is *wow*! We were just soaking in His presence, hearing an answer to prayer. But wait! We are not through—there's more!

Alfred had turned around and started to walk to the altar (platform). We were thinking that this was "our word" for the day. Alfred suddenly turned around and came back.

He waited until he was standing in front of us before he spoke. "The Lord has revealed to me that there is something else the two of you have been praying for. He has shown me that you two have been asking for a *location*. Where are you supposed to be? Where does the Lord want us to be?"

Then this came out of his mouth, "The Lord has told me to tell you that you are to be *here*—here in this community, here in this town, and here in this church!"

By now Leah was weeping heavily, almost dragging me to the ground. We were both overcome by these words. Of course everyone in the church had known us for about nine months, and they all clapped and cheered. Is this for real or what?

This really was new to us. We hadn't ever had someone give us a word like this—especially to have someone know about the things that we had been both praying for, things that only the two of us and the Lord knew. This was powerful to say the least.

The story does not stop here. Two days later, we were having lunch in Bellville and had an opportunity to visit with Alfred again. This time, there was another word that came. He shared that when we moved, we were not to build or buy a new home but that we were to stay debt free. Yes, debt free, and I asked him why.

He said, "The Lord wants you to stay debt free so that when the time comes and He needs to move you, there will not be anything to tie you down or hold you back. That, when He calls, you can pick up and go."

> In all your ways acknowledge Him, and He shall direct your paths. (Prov. 3:6, NKJV)

Wow! All that I can say is *wow*!

So back to Katy we went, praying, talking about the weekend, and praying some more. I then I shared with Leah about the last time that we moved. How I had felt a prompting from the Lord to prepare to move, and I had started packing up the house.

I asked her if she remembered that, back in 1994. She said that she did. I then asked her what she thought of me packing up and getting ready. Her answer was priceless. She said, "I thought you were *nuts*! And *no*! I was not going to help you pack." (And she didn't!)

But three weeks later, after we returned from vacation, a home had come up for rent and we found ourselves moving in only two weeks. We bought that same home six months later and that was where we had lived since then.

This time we both knew that the Lord had answered our prayers and we wanted to be obedient to Him, so by the weekend we were already packing and preparing to move.

We began cleaning and packing and storing everything in boxes. We also had had our good friend Alton come out and start fixing anything that needed to be repaired at the house.

All of our packed items were soon in the garage. On the Tuesday before Thanksgiving, I spoke with our friend and realtor, Ed Blanchfield about selling our home. He came out, and we discussed what we felt the house could sell for. He asked how we came up with the selling price.

We told him that Leah and I were on the back porch talking the week before talking about the house.

Leah said, "How much do you think we can get for the house?" I told her that I had a number but would not tell her. I turned my back on her and started to walk out into the backyard. Leah blurted out a number. I started laughing and turned around. Leah took one look at my face and said, "That is the same number you had, isn't it?"

I replied, "Yep! It is!"

So as we talked to Ed about the house, I shared this with him. "I have asked the Lord to sell the house, and this is the figure He gave Leah and me. I told the Lord that I know He doesn't need my help, but if He could, please sell it quickly because I would not want Him to look bad if it doesn't sell right away."

I also shared with Ed that I told God, "I knew He didn't need my help, but if He could, let it be a cash deal—that way there aren't any finance problems with loans. Also that I still knew that He didn't need my help—but if He could—please let the sale of the house close after the first of the year!"

Ed said that he would do his best. He wasn't sure that any of this could happen, but that he would do what he could on his end. After that, Ed went outside and placed the FOR SALE sign in the front of the yard.

Our contractors and cleaning lady were finally through with the house on Saturday just past noon. Following our instructions from Ed, Leah and I took off for the afternoon and came back later that evening. We found two cards on the counter from realtors.

On Sunday morning, we took off for church in Bellville and stayed there for lunch that afternoon. About 3:00 p.m., we got a call from Ed the realtor.

He said, "I wanted to call you and tell you that we have an offer on the house."

"That is great!" I said.

Ed replied, "No. Praise God we got an offer on the house!"

I replied "Well, praise God!

Ed said, "Yes, praise God. We got an offer from the first person on Saturday. They made a cash offer for what you asked for, and we close right after the first of the year!"

My heart was in my chest by now. Oh my God! What an amazing and incredible thing to happen! I have never seen anything like this in my life! Pinch me! Is this for real or what?

This is just another example in learning to have faith—having faith in Him who provides all things. It may not sound like much, but God is in everything that we do, every step of the way.

And these are just a few ways that we learn in taking steps of faith in our life.

You see, in life we need to learn that each step of faith that we take is an adventure. When we first start out, these steps may seem risky to us. And because of our doubt and lack of faith, we want to rationalize everything. Besides, these steps are more than we can handle! We are unsure of ourselves, and we are just plain scared.

But with the Lord's help, *all* things are possible. Don't take my word for this. Take the Lord's Word on it.

> And looking at them Jesus said to them, "With people this is impossible, but with God all things are possible." (Matt. 19:26, NASB)

With each step of faith that we take, we become bolder and stronger. We have to learn to trust in Him for all things.

I like the way that the Message shares about trusting God:

> Trust God from the bottom of your heart don't try to figure out everything on your own. Listen for God's voice in everything you do, everywhere you go; He's the one who will keep you on track. (Prov. 3: 5–6, MSG)

Miracle on the Hill

Leah

> Then he left the land of the Chaldeans and settled
> in Haran. From there, after his father died, God
> had him move to this country in which you are now
> living.
>
> —Acts 7:4 (NASB)

Brian was "hired out" many times over the years to play his keyboards at various churches when they were in need of a keyboardist. One such church, Christian Faith Church in Bellville, had asked him to play keyboards for them off and on during 2000–2003. Don Bleyl, the main guitarist for the Daystar Project Band, had been a big help in getting Brian for those times when they needed someone to play the keyboards for the services there.

In October of 2008, Pastor Lynn Burling of Christian Faith Church in Bellville contacted Brian about having the Daystar Project band come out and lead the whole service. This would mean that they would provide the worship music, a prayer time at the altar, *and* Brian would bring a sermon.

This was a big step of faith because it was the first time that Brian had been asked to preach, as well as bring our music ministry band for the whole service!

In fact, this was one of the first times that he had been asked to preach at a church! It seemed as though Brian worked on that sermon for *weeks*! Everything had to be "*just so.*"

The band had been practicing to get prepared as well, so Brian was really busy getting ready. He was so excited to be able not only to share his music with the church body, but also to bring the sermon.

When he was finished writing out what he wanted to say in the message, he asked me to listen to him and give him some feedback. It was very important to have everything right because we really liked the Bellville church, and the people were wonderful!

After he finished his draft, I listened to the message and gave him a few pointers. He had done a great job! Then he practiced and practiced his sermon, and I was a ready listener.

This would be the beginning of many more sermons where I would help Brian with editing his message and listening while he practiced.

The day finally arrived. We took the scenic drive from our home in Katy to Bellville and met with the rest of the band at the church for a final run-through of the music. We worked until just a few minutes before the start of the service. Then we went into a small room, sat down together with the pastor, and prayed for the band, for Brian, and for God's presence in the service. This was a special time of relaxing in God's presence and preparing our hearts for the service.

Then it was off to the sanctuary to lead worship and hear Brian preach! All of us were excited to be there and to lead the congregation in worship as the Lord allowed. The worship set was awesome, and then Pastor Lynn introduced Brian. As he walked up to the platform, I was praying for him to be open and to let the Lord lead him.

> Ascribe to the Lord the glory due His name; bring an offering, and come before Him; Worship the Lord in holy array. (1 Chron. 16:29, NASB)

Brian looked so relaxed and ready to go. He began to share with the people, and I felt the presence of the Lord in that place. It was really great! At the end of the service, there was a time of commitment where people could come to the front and pray or have someone pray with and for them. There were several who came forward. Donna (our lead singer) and I were busy praying with them for a while. It was really neat to see how the people had been touched by the Lord.

After the service, we adjourned to the fellowship hall to have lunch, which had been provided by the ladies at the church. It was really nice, and we felt very much at home there. These people were *so* very sweet and made us all feel like we belonged.

Brian and I continued to visit Christian Faith Church for the next few weeks. It was kind of funny that each time we walked into the church, somebody would always ask us, "Why are you here?" We would laugh and say that we felt drawn to the church, the pastor, and the people there. It was true, and we were coming to the church because we felt the presence of the Lord there.

After several months, we felt the stirring of the Lord and believed that it might be time for us to consider a move to Bellville or somewhere in that area. We began to come out to Bellville each week, working with a realtor who took us to various houses that were for rent within forty miles of the church. We looked at all types of homes, some really big and very costly (even to rent!), and some very tiny; even a couple that were in disrepair, or basically unliveable.

We were honest with the realtors and told them that we were looking but did not know what we wanted. We did not want them to waste a great deal of time in helping us to find the right home when we were not sure ourselves.

Our realtor was beginning to get discouraged because we seemed to be looking and looking but had not found anything yet. We were beginning to get a bit discouraged as well. Finally, we told the realtor that we just weren't ready to move yet. I think he was probably relieved: now he could work with some "real" prospects!

During this time, we had been getting our home in Katy ready to sell. It actually sold on the first day for exactly the asking price! We were so glad, however it created a *big* challenge for us. We now had to find a place to live quickly. We had to be completely out of our Katy house in *three weeks*! Yikes! It was a strange position that we were in now. We had been told by the Lord not to buy or build a house and to stay debt free. Wow! This was a huge step of faith for both Brian and me!

With our prayers answered and the house sold, and the clock ticking on our three weeks, we *had* to find a place to live immediately.

One day while we were in Bellville, we wandered into a different realtor's office, just to see what they had to offer. The agent was very nice, and she showed us a couple of properties that were available to rent. Then just as we were turning to leave, she stopped us and asked, "Do you know where the town of New Ulm is?"

Brian replied, "Yes, I do." He had played golf a couple of times at the New Ulm golf course, The Falls.

The realtor said she had a listing for a house for rent out that way and, if we wanted to go look at it, she would notify the owners. When she contacted Mary, the owner, she learned that Mary was already at the house cleaning. Mary told her to tell us to "Come on out!"

The trip out to New Ulm was scenic but it seemed like a long drive from Bellville, especially when we left the paved road and drove on a dirt road. However, in due time we were on the road where the rental house was located. While

Brian drove, I was holding the picture of the house and looking for it as we drove…further and further out into the country. It seemed to be "forever"!

> But if from there you seek the Lord your God, you will find him if you seek him with all your heart and with all your soul. (Deut. 4:29, NIV)

All of a sudden, Brian heard me say loudly, "*Stop*! Here it is! Here's the house!"

He looked out and said, "That just can't be the house… it's so big!"

I shook my head and said, "Look at the picture! It's the house! It's the house!"

This reaction was very similar to the movie *Miracle on 34th Street* (a Christmas movie classic), where a young Natalie Wood was looking for a house that she had told Santa she wanted. When she and her parents were driving down the road, young Natalie began to yell at her parents to "Stop the car! There's the house! *There's the house*!"

Brian laughed and then pulled into the drive.

As we turned into the property, Mary came out to greet us. We introduced ourselves and entered the house. All I could think was, *Wow!*

The house *was* quite large, especially for just two people (and four cats), but it was so "homey," so comfortable. Mary gave us the tour, telling us about her family: her husband and their six boys.

It now made sense to us why the house was so big. We had a laugh about it and went upstairs to see the bedrooms. She told us that they had actually moved this house from across the pasture behind where we were now by putting it on a flatbed trailer and *towing* it across the fields to its final resting place here. Mary and her family had built a new house for themselves and decided to put this one up for rent. I think her plan was that when one of her boys got married, they might want to live here, close to her.

Once upstairs, we looked at the four bedrooms while Mary shared about their time in the house. We all walked into the master bedroom, continuing to talk. Brian began to share with Mary about our lives, losing Victoria, and feeling a tug to move out of Katy—out to the country. Within minutes, both Mary and I were in tears.

We laughed about it, and then discussed the rent, and anything else we could think of. Both Brian and I were very comfortable with Mary, and she was with us as well. We had more discussion and told Mary we needed to pray about it, and we would let her know if we had God's permission to rent the house.

Before we left to drive back to Katy, Brian took a few minutes to walk out the back door onto the back porch. A few minutes later he slowly came back inside, tears in his eyes. Both Mary and I were surprised and asked what was wrong.

Brian shared that as he stepped out to the edge of the back porch, he saw his "safe place" while looking out over the fields. This was something that our counselor had helped each of us find during our sessions with her after our daughter had died. She would tell us (individually) to close our eyes, and think of a "safe place" to be—somewhere that was peaceful and quiet, and then go there in our minds. *Wow*! That was quite a confirmation for both Brian and me!

> Trust in the Lord and do good; dwell in the land and enjoy safe pasture. (Ps. 37:3)

Once on the road back to our house in Katy, Brian and I talked nonstop about the house on the hill. Both of us really loved it, as well as the location. (Who *wouldn't* love it?) When we got back home, we worked on our budget and decided that we just might be able to swing the rent. We were very excited. But of course, before we could make that final decision, we would need to pray, pray, pray for God's direction.

Brian and I had learned over the years that God desires to be part of *everything* in our lives. He is not an absent God. He is our Father in heaven. He loves us. Because of that, Brian and I began to pray about the house in the country. After a couple of days, both of us had a peace about that home and let Mary, our new landlord, know. She was glad for us, and of course, we were really happy.

Next came all the packing. Brian had already done a great deal of packing with our friends from Bellville—Lauren, Benjamin, and another young man named Sudeep. It was hard work to get everything ready to go, but we had fun doing it. Finally we were ready to get moving. It was January 2, 2010, and we were ready to go!

Brian and I hadn't decided whether to use a large moving van service or rent a large truck to move our household out to the new house. Then, one Sunday at the church, we were surprised and delighted when Dawn, one of our new friends at Christian Faith Church in Bellville, stepped in and basically solved the entire moving situation by "volunteering" the men of the church to help us. They would provide trucks and manpower to get us loaded up in Katy, then unpack everything at the new house. On top of that, Dawn provided lunch for everyone.

What a *great* way to get moved. Woo-hoo!

The crew that came to our house in Katy loaded everything including our four cats. Then we drove to New Ulm and the new house. It was a crazy day for everyone, but we got through it. Brian and I slept for the first time in our house in the country that night. It was awesome.

Brian and I had already named our new home The Hill, because the house is located on top of…a hill. (Duh!) We have lived out here on The Hill ever since then and still love it. We can look out from our back porch and see rolling hills and pastures. We also can watch cattle grazing right next to our yard. It's such a serene and beautiful place to live.

We are constantly thanking our Father in heaven for such a marvelous place to live. He is always willing to give us His best when we let Him be an intimate part of our lives. Looking out the back windows of the house, we are constantly reminded of His gentle and loving care. He cares about what we think, what we feel, what we want. He always desires to show His love and care to His dear children. We can almost feel His arms around us at times, just letting us know that He loves us.

This whole thing was a *huge* step of faith for me, but especially for Brian. It was really awesome to see God move—*here* and *now!* This would become just one of many steps of faith that the Lord would show us—there is much more.

If *you* don't know Jesus—really know Jesus as Savior and Lord—you only need to look at His beautiful creations! Remember, *we* are also His creations, which is why we look for someone greater than we are that we may *love Him back!* I can only tell you that *you are not alone!* GOD is great and He must be praised! Reach out to Him through prayers, or simply by asking Him to show Himself to you, and He will. Look at the world that He made, simply by *speaking* it into being. God is amazing, creative, and loving. If you do not know him yet, simply *ask* Him to show you Who He is, or ask a pastor, or a friend.

You are loved by the God Who made you in your mother's womb. He desires a close, personal relationship with all of His children. Why not *you*? Why not *now*?

> The Lord is my shepherd; I shall not want. He makes me to lie down in green pastures; He leads me beside the still waters.
>
> He restores my soul; He leads me in the paths of righteousness for His name's sake.
>
> Yea, though I walk through the valley of the shadow of death, I will fear no evil; for You are with me; Your rod and Your staff, they comfort me.
>
> You prepare a table before me in the presence of my enemies; You anoint my head with oil; my cup runs over.
>
> Surely goodness and mercy shall follow me all the days of my life; And I will dwell in the house of the Lord forever. (Psalm 23, NKJV)

The Journey Toward Healing

Leah

> Consider it pure joy, my brothers and sisters,
> whenever you face trials of many kinds, because
> you know that the testing of your faith produces
> perseverance. Let perseverance finish its work so
> that you may be mature and complete, not lacking
> anything. If any of you lacks wisdom, you should ask
> God, who gives generously to all without finding
> fault, and it will be given to you.
>
> —James 1:2–5 (NIV)

There are many things we go through during our lives. Sometimes these are really wonderful; sometimes they are really horrible things. However, we learn from each and every thing that we go through. Our goal, therefore, is not to avoid going through anything, but to try and learn from whatever we come across.

It is the same with trials and tribulations: we usually don't ask for them, but we receive them anyway. I believe that God puts these things into our lives to grow us, to help us learn, and to strengthen us in this life. Many times these trials are fairly simple ones that don't require much on our part except to accept them and move on. At other times a trial can be almost more than we can bear. Such was the case when Brian and I lost our daughter Victoria in 2004.

You might think that our story ended then and there. In one sense, it did; in another, it opened up a whole new world for both Brian and me. Our story took a drastic turn on the pathway of our lives, one which neither of us could have ever seen coming. Our only daughter murdered, and our faith in Christ rocked to the very core. We were truly unable to function.

During this time, we began to pray and ask God things such as "Why? God, are You *really* there?" as well as many others. It was pretty tough in those first hours. For us, however, the first thing we both did, separately and then together, was to throw ourselves into our Father God's lap and beg Him to make some sense of this tragedy.

> I lift up my eyes to the hills. From where does my help come? My help comes from the Lord, who made heaven and earth. (Ps. 121:1–2, ESV)

It is difficult to explain exactly what Brian and I felt. Our world as we knew it had broken. The *only* thing we could do was pray and ask God, "Why?" Within about forty-eight hours, we had our answer. God covered both of us with His "peace that passes all understanding." We absolutely *knew* where our daughter was. We *knew* that God was in charge. We also realized that with Him, we would be okay. What a change!

I remember a feeling of being released, of being assured that God *was* in control and that He *would* take care of us. His love was sufficient for us then and is still sufficient today. Brian and I have come through the fire and been able to overcome a trial that might have ended in depression, in divorce, or in the death of our future together. Because He is our God, we have learned to live again, and to glorify Him in everything we do. We have seen the healing of hearts and lives today because of our Lord Jesus. Amen!

> But to each one of us grace was given according to the measure of Christ's gift. (Eph. 4:7, NKJV)

In the years since our sweet girl left this world for the *best* one, Brian and I have gone through many, many challenges. One of the most difficult was beginning to live again after her death. God became our total focus; He led us to the healing of our marriage, through wonderful Christian counseling that pointed us to Him and to the healing of our broken hearts.

Ultimately, God gave us a "job" that only with His power and strength could we fulfill. He began sending us to other families who have lost children—families whose lives have been slammed up against a wall of pain and suffering. Because we can understand *exactly* what they are going through, we are able to give them some good tools to use to begin to live again. First, we point them straight to our great Savior, and then we give them some practical pointers on how to move on and begin to heal from this tragedy.

In our visits with these devastated families, we bring to them the empathy of someone who has gone through *exactly* what they are going through. There is nothing more precious than seeing these broken family members realize that we *do* understand what they are feeling and that we can show them ways to help their walk down this road!

However, our God is greater than any of us can imagine. His plans are much, much larger than we can dream. In 2007, as he was sleeping, Brian heard the Voice of God telling him that he would write a book, and that the name of the book was to be *From Misery to Ministry*. Well, as Brian would tell you, his reaction was to try to ignore that prompting from God and go back to sleep. However, God is persistent. Again Brian heard that Voice telling him to write a book called *From Misery to Ministry*—and to "*Get up and write it down now!*"

> Then the Lord said to me, "Write my answer plainly on tablets, so that a runner can carry the correct message to others." (Hab. 2:2, NLT)

From that nighttime encounter came the book *From Misery to Ministry—A Walk of Faith for Those Who Have Lost a Loved One*. It was released in June of 2011 by Tate Publishing and has been a wonderful tool to help families who have lost a loved one, especially a child.

In the book, Brian and I take turns sharing our feelings as well as what God taught us during the time after Victoria died. We share from our hearts and explain how God was the *only* hope that we had during that time. Through the pages of the book, I believe that people can come to realize that our God is greater than anything in this world, and He is the hope that we need.

And, now, God has prompted Brian and me to begin a second book, and to call it *Steps of Faith.* We are to share some of the many, many encounters we have had as we walk according to His direction. During this time, we have met and ministered to so many hurting people. Because of our openness to follow His leading, we too have been abundantly blessed. Believe me, there is nothing more precious than spending time with someone who has been devastated by the loss of a loved one, and then to see them realize that they are *not* alone in this trial; that the Father God, who *also* lost a child, is with them during this difficult time, and He sent Brian and me to help them walk down the road to healing.

We are blessed to be able to minister to others in Jesus' Name! Only He can—and has—given us the words and the heart to help others walk through this time of unbelievable pain and suffering. Only with Him can they be truly healed!

Our ministry was started to help those who have been devastated or who have lost their way through the sorrow of losing a child or anyone who is dear to them. Through our Lord, we can point them to Him to help them find the healing that they might have never found otherwise.

The Lord has also opened many doors for us, with churches. We give them another resource to help minister to their congregation and reach out to families in the community.

God is our Provider, He is our Healer, He is our All-in-All. Not one of us would be here if we were not meant to be here. By our acceptance of Jesus Christ as our Savior, we have been adopted into the Family of God, an adoption that can *never* be reversed! Through Jesus and His sacrifice for us, we have learned that we can go on, we can be happy again, and we can follow the paths that God has laid out for us.

> For, you did not receive the spirit of bondage again to fear, but you received the Spirit of adoption, by whom we cry out Abba, Father. (Rom. 8:15, NKJV)

Remember, God knows *exactly* how we feel; He lost His child too! However, in His great loss, God gained many, many "children" because of the sacrifice made by Jesus.

What Jesus has done can never be reversed, and we are confident that we will be with our Lord in heaven one day. Brian likes to tell people that with God a day is like a thousand years. If that is the case, our Victoria has gone out to play, and when she gets back to her heavenly home, we will be there waiting for her. Then we will all be together again, praising our mighty Lord and King forever!

Peace I leave with you, My peace I give to you; not as the world gives do I give to you. Let not your heart be troubled, neither let it be afraid. (John 14:27, NKJV)

God's Special Gifts

Leah and Brian

> So shall My word be that goes forth out of My mouth: it shall not return to Me void [without producing any effect, useless], but it shall accomplish that which I please and purpose, and it shall prosper in the thing for which I sent it.
>
> —Isaiah 55:11 (AMP)

We have found, like most other people who have lost a child or a loved one, that you go through a time of grieving. You grieve not only the loss of the loved one, but you begin to feel that there is a *big* hole in your life.

You say to yourself, "Something is missing!" It feels strange, and you have emptiness that needs to be filled up. Yes, I want it filled up with something or anything. Just fill it up!

That feeling is a void in your life and it can only be totally filled by one person. And that person is our Lord Jesus Christ.

Don't get me wrong. There are things that you can do to fill in the blank or the void spot. You can decide to become really busy with your life, your work, or your hobby. But only God can fill that void completely.

In time, the other options will burn you out emotionally, and you will have to find something else to try to fill that void. But after it is all said and done, in the end that void will only be truly filled by Him.

God will fill this void when we turn to Jesus and trust Him.

Even in times of trouble and distress, the Lord still has a plan for us.

> O LORD, You are my God; I will exalt You, I will give thanks to Your name; For You have worked wonders, Plans formed long ago, with perfect faithfulness. (Is. 25:1, NASB)

Leah and I found ourselves with that void for a brief period of time.

Let me share with you how God provided an answer to our prayers.

During our years of marriage and after Victoria was born, the Lord would provide additional "daughters" on loan from God.

These daughters would come from the girls that Victoria went to school with and those she met at church and in the neighborhood.

At times, it seemed like we did not go anywhere that we did not have three or four girls in tow with us. Sometimes people would ask us if these were all our children. When they did, we would just laugh and say, "Yes, they are all with us!"

A number of these girls over the years would call us "Mom" and "Dad" because they always felt at ease with us, and our place just felt like home.

We still stay in touch of some of those girls today. Many have grown up, gotten married, and started having children. Though we do not see them or hear from them often, the memories are still with us to this day.

Since our daughter Victoria died in 2004, God has mercifully given us great relationships with other young women who bless our lives. These "special gifts" from God have been such a blessing for Leah and me.

> Behold, children are a gift of the Lord, the fruit of the womb is the reward. (Ps. 127:3, NASB)

One of those special gifts was a young girl named April.

Leah shares it best: "While our daughter Victoria was alive, she had a very special best friend named April. April's family lived fairly close to our house. As Victoria would tell us, 'We were *instant* best friends!' April and Victoria were constantly together, unless they were at school or somewhere with their families. It seemed to us that we never saw one without the other. Those two were nearly inseparable.

"It was at this time, like all best friends, that April got a special name from us. We would simply call her *Lirpa*. That is her named spelled backwards.

"Vic and April would do many things together. Whenever possible, we would take Lirpa with us on vacations—especially to see Aunt Marta in Atlanta."

Later, when Victoria was older, she added some new and different friends who began to coax her down the wrong path. April told Victoria that she would not hang out with her if she was with those friends.

A friend once asked us about April's decision. Leah gave this wonderful reply. "It must have been hard for April to tell Victoria that and hard for Victoria to hear it. However, Vic accepted that there were 'boundaries' with their friendship. They did spend some time together, although not as much as before. I think Victoria always felt sad about that, but April's decision was firm."

Talking with Leah on one of our drives, I asked her how she felt about this void with no children in the house. My bride gave me this wonderful response. "After Vic's death, our house seems to be pretty empty because there aren't any of Vic's friends around. You know, our other kids."

However, April did come by the house from time to time. I remember that on one occasion she shared with us that Victoria would sometimes call her to come and pick her up from wherever she was. Apparently, the "friends" Victoria was spending time with would sometimes refuse to bring her back home, and she'd have to find a ride or walk home. When that happened, she'd call April to come and get her.

April was extremely worried by the type of friends that Victoria had chosen to spend time with, concerned that Victoria might get hurt.

In reality, Victoria *was* being hurt by how these "friends" would treat her. This included stealing from her, leaving her stranded at night, and ultimately taking her life!

Leah would later go on to say, "When Victoria passed, I remember when April came to us one day and shared that she would always be there for us and that we were part of her family. What a wonderful promise to be made by a young woman who was our daughter's best friend."

When it came time for the murder trial the following year after Victoria's death, April came to Leah and said, "I am going to go to the trial with you." April was a senior in high school that year, and Leah was concerned about the details of the trial and how it would affect her. Leah told April that she needed to run this past her mother and get permission. April's response was classic: "I will ask my mother, but *I am still going!*"

She wanted to be there for Victoria, and she wanted to be there for Leah and me—but mostly for Leah. It was like having another daughter there to walk through that difficult season all as one family. She was not only a blessing to us, but she was a special gift by God to minister to us.

April continues to be part of our lives today. We visit with her several times each year. She will cut our hair and spend some time at lunch whenever possible. As I like to share with others, I pay a lot for a haircut. It is just a small way to bless her in the way that she has blessed us. I remember April telling me one time, "You do not have to write me a check every time you see me!"

My response came quickly, "April, we love you, and we want to bless you. Besides, if Victoria were still alive, we would be writing her these checks!" At first she looked stunned, then she smiled, gave me a big long hug, and told me that she loved us. That's my girl!

It's an awesome feeling to know that April is just as glad to see *us* as we are to see *her*. To this day, she still seems like a daughter to us.

I would like to share another story with you on how God's special gifts came about, but I need to set this up for you.

In the summer of 1999, I began to play music again. In time, with the help of some friends, we started a new Christian music group called The Daystar Project. We were a grand experience in Christian music.

On New Year's Eve in 1999, The Daystar Project was asked to play for a midnight service to welcome in the New Year at Christian Faith Church in Bellville, Texas.

Victoria and Leah drove out to the church to hear the group. It was an awesome evening of praise and worship. After that time, I began to be invited to assist with the praise team occasionally. Our good friend Don Bleyl, who played guitar, had suggested that I come out and play with the praise team, and the people at the church were thrilled to have me come.

After that first service, Leah and I began to visit Christian Faith Church from time to time. It was a wonderful little church. Don would invite me to come out on Saturday, to rehearsal, and to play with the praise band on Sunday morning.

After Victoria died, it would about four years before we would make it back to Christian Faith Church.

Our group was asked to take the entire service one Sunday in November 2008. The ministry band provided the worship music and time at the altar, and I (Brian) was honored to bring the sermon message for that morning. It was awesome.

In 2009 we began visiting the church on a regular basis. By October we were given a word that we would be moving to the Austin County area. This would be another step of faith for us. But we will share more on that later.

During this time, we met a young couple named Benjamin and Lauren.

Lauren was several years younger than Victoria would have been, and God had something special in store for all of us. She would be a special love gift from God.

Lauren seemed to be drawn to Leah from the very first time they met, and she continued to spend quality time with us every time we were at church. At first, we did not know what to think of this, then God began to show us something special.

They say that a picture is worth a thousand words. Well, let me paint a word picture for you.

It was the funniest thing. Lauren began to do something that was very much like what our Victoria would do.

Lauren would come up to Leah, regardless of where Leah was sitting, and simply plop into her lap, place her arms around her neck and say, "Mom (or Mommy), I love you!"

The very first time this happened, I was up on the stage platform playing my keyboard. When I looked out into the congregation, I saw Leah. She had this bright red nose, a smile, and some tears running down her cheeks.

As we continued visiting the church each Sunday, Lauren unknowingly began to do the same thing on a regular basis with Leah.

I always knew when Lauren had done that because I'd look out from the stage and see Leah with a red nose and a smile.

Over time, Lauren and Benjamin would become good friends with us. It was like have a daughter and a son–in-law, but more like a daughter and son.

When the time came for us to move, they came to our house and helped us pack up and prepare for the move.

On one of their visits, we were packing games and other items from some of the rooms. I decided to ask Lauren if she would like some of Victoria's things. We felt that this would be just a small payment for helping us with the move.

She said, "Sure." So off we all went down the hall toward Victoria's room.

While Lauren and I were in Victoria's room, I told Lauren that I had something that we wanted to give her but was not sure if she would want it. Victoria, you see, had this blue jean jacket with fake fur on the sleeves and on the liner inside the jacket. All of her friends loved that jacket, and Vic seemed to wear it almost everywhere that she went when it was cool outside. Someone had the coat dry-cleaned for us and it had been in the closet for some time.

When I pulled the coat out, I said, "Do you think you might want this?" Lauren's eyes opened really wide and, starring intensely at the coat, she said, "Ooh, yeah!" It was like watching someone get something they always wanted.

Later in December, when the time came for us to move, I shared with the church that we were now planning to move to New Ulm, Texas. This is a town on the far west side of Austin County, about twenty miles from Bellville.

When I shared that our house had been sold and that we had to move soon, God provided another cool provision in our step of faith. Trusting Him is always number one!

After sharing about us preparing to move to the area, Dawn, one of the church ladies, came up to me and asked how we were going to move. I told her, "We love our friends, so we will be paying someone to move us from Katy to New Ulm."

Dawn was wonderful and then suddenly spoke directly to us. "No, you don't! We got lots of men here with trucks, trailers, and we have a horse trailer that we can use. We'll take care of getting you moved up here. And don't worry about feeding them, I will take care of everything." Wow! Go, God!

After we moved to the country, Benjamin and Lauren came out for a visit to the house on The Hill. They helped us with some more unpacking and had dinner. Then they got ready to go home.

It had been really cold that day and Benjamin's truck did not have a heater, so when they got ready to leave I offered Lauren a blanket. It was one of Leah's that had a southwestern design to it.

Several weeks later, Leah asked Lauren at church if the blanket had been warm enough for her. She said it was just right.

Joking with her a bit, I said, "So, would you like to keep the blanket?"

To which came this reply, "Oh, yes! I want to keep it… it smells like Leah."

Leah almost cried on the spot. Leah later shared with me, "This was so sweet of her—she really likes us—it is like we were becoming her spiritual parents, or aunt and uncle!"

God really knows how much Leah and I want to have a family—one that loves us and really likes to spend time with us.

I want to turn back the clock for a moment and share something special with you.

Right after Victoria died in March of 2004, our band was recording a CD at Grace UMC in Katy. One night I got to the church early to practice when suddenly God gave me a new song. I played through it a couple of times, then went to the back of the church and started the recorder. I came back up to the stage and recorded the song. I called it "The Dance."

I could actually see Victoria in my mind, dancing to this song. Later a friend of ours said this would be a great song for an ice skater to skate to. Leah loves this song, and when I play it in church, she cries. Now, this is not to make her sad; it's a reminder of our girl and the fun things she did— how she would dance as a child. This is always a *good* cry.

Okay, so let me get back to the special moment at Christian Faith Church.

At one evening service, people were lined up across the front of the altar. Pastor Lynn was praying for different people. As I played "The Dance," another special God-moment arrived.

I saw Lauren get up and cross from the other side of the sanctuary to where Leah was sitting and began to sit down.

Leah scooted over to let her sit down next to her. But Lauren did not sit next to Leah. Instead, she crawled gently over the side and sat down in Leah's lap just like Victoria used to. Then she put her arms around her neck and laid her head down on Leah's shoulder. They both hugged one another and cried. It was such a tender moment to watch.

Leah then looked up at me, with her red nose and tears and a smile of gladness and love on her face. It was very special to see.

God had given Lauren the spirit of love and the ability to know just the right buttons to push on Leah.

Leah later shared with me that Lauren had called her "Mom" earlier in the day. What a blessing she has been and continues to be for the two of us!

We need to remember that it is God's love that fills us up. His word *never* lies, *never* changes and is *always* true, and only *he* can fill that void. What an awesome God we serve!

> The Lord your God is with you; His power gives you victory. The Lord will take delight in you, and in His love He will give you new life. He will sing and be joyful over you. (Zeph. 3:17 GNT)

Pizza in His Presence

Leah

> "Preach the word of God. Be prepared, whether the
> time is favorable or not. Patiently correct, rebuke, and
> encourage your people with good teaching."
>
> —2 Timothy 4:2 (NLT)

On most Wednesday nights, Brian and I eat at a local pizza parlor before attending our church's Wednesday night Bible study group. One Wednesday, we entered the establishment, and one of the young ladies took our "regular" order.

I took a copy of a local monthly newspaper inside the restaurant to give to the owner and to leave it there for anyone who might wish to read it. On the front page of the paper was an article about our ministry and how we got where we are today. Our waitress, Masey took the paper and went back to prepare our pizza as Brian and I sat down at a table to wait.

We sat talking for a few minutes, and then Masey came out from the kitchen to our table. She looked as if she was having trouble choosing words to say. Finally she said, "I was just now reading your story in this paper and just had to come out here and tell you how sorry I am that you lost your daughter. I know that you two are Christians, as am I, and I'm getting ready to leave for college.

"I am concerned that when I get to college and away from my family and my church home, I might be sucked into all that *stuff* that goes on at college, and I might not stay close to the Lord. Do you have any advice that you can give to me, to help me stay on the right path?"

Well, that was kind of like telling a hunting dog, "Okay boy, sic 'em!"

Both of us looked at one another and smiled. "Of course," we said, smiling at Masey. We then told her about some of the things we had experienced when we were in college, and how the Lord has told us that He will never leave us nor forsake us if we trust in Him to guide us. We told her some things that our daughter had been involved in during the time when she was far from the Lord, and about how she turned her life around just before her death. We also shared that we both believe that Jesus was right there with her at the very moment of death to take her to her eternal home with Him.

Then we visited with Masey for a few more minutes, encouraging her to read her Bible daily and to pick friends who were also Christ-confessing Christians. She needed to find one or two girls with similar beliefs at college or at church who would be accountability partners with and for her. These special friends would hold Masey accountable for her actions away from home, and she would do the same for them.

We told her that we had not come into the pizza place by chance that night; it was what we call a "divine appointment," and that she was so special to God that He gave her the courage to come out and really talk to us. Isn't our God great? We ended our conversation by giving Masey our email addresses so she could keep in touch when she left for school.

This divine appointment is just one of many others that we have been given over the past few years. God is always willing to "send" us someone who needs Him, His guidance, or His message. All we need to do is be willing to act on His behalf!

Where Did That Come From?

Brian

> There is an appointed time for everything. And there
> is a time for every event under heaven.
>
> —Ecclesiastes 3:1 (NASB)

Have you ever found yourselves working on project, a marketing idea, or a plan design "new for the ages"?

We all find ourselves at some point planning something or doing something, and suddenly—from out of nowhere—this amazing and incredible idea comes into your mind. You think to yourself, "Wow! How cool is that! Look what I just came up with!"

Okay, did you come up with that idea all by yourself? Think again.

> Every good thing given and every perfect gift is from
> above, coming down from the Father of lights, with
> whom there is no variation or shifting shadow. (James
> 1:17, NASB)

When we walk through life, we wonder why some things happen. Something unexpected happens, and we ask ourselves:

- What is happening?

- Where is this going?
- Is this something that I will use now or later?

All good questions, my friend Stephen Coffee would say. Yes, these are all good questions.

When I was just four years old my mother, a very talented and gifted music teacher, started me on the path of music. She started me first on the piano, then the organ, and then the accordion. Yes, the "squeezebox."

Someone once joked with me and asked me, "What is the true definition of a gentleman?" I said, "I don't know," to which came this reply: "A true gentleman is a man who can play the accordion but won't!"

A few years later, my mother started me on the violin. This did not last long. Ha! After that came the flute. That too did not last very long. But in my 6th grade year, my sister came home with a tenor saxophone. Shazam! "That's for me!" I shouted.

Over the next several years I learned to play the baritone sax, the bass sax, and the alto sax. Then I was given lessons on the guitar, then singing, and even classes on the basics to write music. I tried college for a couple of years but dropped out and went to work. Then I just stopped playing.

Twenty years later God would begin to give me my music back.

You see, we are all born with certain gifts and talents. For me, the Father had blessed me with a gift of music.

When I turned thirty years of age, He gave me the most important special gift of all. That was the gift of eternal life when I proclaimed Jesus Christ as my personal Savior.

Then, when I turned fifty, the Father showed me another gift. It was one that I did not know that I had. That would be the gift of encouragement, through both words and music.

It would not be until the death of our only daughter, Victoria, that the Lord gave me a passion for music and a desire to light the fire in the belly of the church through music.

During this time, I realized some very important things about life, and about the *steps of faith* that we take. Sometimes, we do not realize that we are actually taking these steps of faith—but surprise! We are!

> For I know the plans that I have for you, declares the Lord, plans for welfare and not for calamity to give you a future and a hope. (Jer. 29:11, NASB)

As I continued writing music and seeking Him more and more, God was slowly revealing more to me with the new steps in my faith. These steps would become evident in time.

Let me share with you how this happened.

My new journey in music found me only playing Christian music and hymns. This was a twist from my days of playing music from groups like Blood Sweat and Tears,

Chicago, Issac Hayes and The Grass Roots, along with jazz and some classical.

I was writing and arranging Christian music, mostly for our group The Daystar Project. But behind the scenes, something interesting began to happen. The Lord began to give me some very passionate instrumental music. At first, that music seemed only to be between the Lord and me. I played it to be pleasing to Him.

In 1999, while taking my first baby steps into music ministry, the Lord gave me a song to remind me of His promises for now and the future.

Our group would play this song from time to time. I always wanted to record this song, but it never seemed to fit with the other songs in the worship playlists.

As time drifted by, I would often wonder what would happen to the song of His Promises.

Would it ever be recorded, or would it always be on the "back burner," as musicians like to say? Like bread, some songs just never rise to the top and are ready for use.

But the words the Lord gave me never left me.

"For the Breath of God fills my life with love and gives me joy to praise His name. And I freely give to you all the desires of my heart. And I give you to you all my praise and adoration!"

During this time, my good friend Don Bleyl, an amazing and anointed guitarist, would play some of my "little ditty" songs with me. One of these songs was a nice piano piece in the classical genre called "Don's Song." I gave it this name because I played it with Don.

We would talk about the song. Don would ask, "What's with this song?" I would tell him, "It's nice to play and fun, but I just don't see where this will ever be recorded and used for anything!" But God had other plans. Wait for it.

Over the next several years, the Lord would give me some amazing arrangements of songs that had been written by other great artists. Some were hymns and some were original songs.

Our music ministry was "a grand experience (and experiment) in Christian Music." Most of the time it was fun: we were always doing something new and different with music. Changes in the band's musicians also kept things interesting.

These times were also steps of faith for me as I learned to write and be led by His Spirit, but also for those within the group, as well as those who came and listened to God's music.

Hearts and lives changed when we played! The music would bring new hope to musicians that had been burned out and inspire worship leaders giving them new ideas for their choir, orchestra, or praise band. God is always at work. Most of the people in our group were in their late 40s to mid and late 50s. God can still use you at any age!

Our violinist, Carolyn Burrell, who had suffered a terrible injury, lived her life in a wheel chair. As a professional musician, most of her playing was for paid gigs with professional orchestras—weddings, special events, and string ensembles.

Our group was a huge step for her into the area of contemporary Christian music, full of fun and creativity. She would ask me, "Do you have any music for me to read? What do you want me to play?"

I told her, "Play whatever the Lord gives you." She would then scribble a note on her music page. "Play somethin'!" And, boy, did she ever!

She wrote some of the most amazing violin parts to our music—all styles of music. She sang and played. You could see the Glory of God in her face and hear it in her music. She was amazing and anointed!

With her testimony and faith, she gave many people hope and was an inspiration to young people and those starting out on violin. She was jazzed to be on the set with God. And that was a big Step. With Him *all* things are possible. Though Carolyn could not physically walk, she learned to take steps of faith in her daily walk. In time, the rest of the band learned to take steps of faith in their walks with the Lord.

> Speak out to one another in psalms and hymns and spiritual songs, offering praise with voices [and instruments] and making melody with all your heart to the Lord (Eph. 5:19, AMP)

When our daughter Victoria died in 2004, my whole world was shaken and my music changed. The first step came when Leah and I began to talk about Vic's service.

I asked Leah, "Do you think we should find somebody to do the music for the service?" Leah said, "What do you think?" To which I replied, "I think I would like for The Daystar Project to do the music as a tribute to Victoria."

Leah's response: "You should do it. It will bring glory and honor to Him!"

Leah and I prayed about the songs that we wanted for the service. She said, "One song that you have to play is 'As the Deer,' and I want Carolyn to play the violin with you. That is my one request."

"Okay," I said.

The music in the service was both anointed and amazing. God's presence was everywhere. You could actually feel Him right there in the service. We played some worship songs of well-known Christian contemporary artists, along with creative arrangements of hymns. We also played some original songs that the Lord had given me to write. I felt like we had been playing for an audience of "One." A true worship service before the King.

When the service was over Leah, along with her family, were then escorted out into the foyer to be greeted by the congregation as they left. The band then played an arrangement of "When I Survey the Wondrous Cross" in an uplifting Celtic style. You could almost feel the people dance out of the sanctuary. It was powerful!

A good friend of ours, Harry Herzog came up to the front and just stood there while we played. His mouth was half opened, his eyes just stared to the front, and a smile of peace was on his face.

When we finished playing, he came up to me and said, "My God…I just don't know how you could do that! To play! I could not have done that!"

My response: "It's all God."

From that point on there was passion in my music. There was life, hope, encouragement, and zeal!

That summer, our music group was preparing to work on a recording project, our first worship CD. I got to rehearsal at Grace UMC early one evening and set everything up so that we could hit the ground running as soon as everyone arrived.

I went up to the stage and began to play my keyboard, and suddenly, out of nowhere, this song came into my head. I could not shake it. The more and more that my fingers touched the keys, the more melody line the Lord gave me, and the more that I played. The Lord gave me a "road map" on what to play. In music terms, that would be a verse of a song and then a chorus of the song.

Since I did not want to lose this new creation, I jumped up and ran down to the recording booth. I hit the record button for my instrument. The recording program was now running live. Quickly I ran back up to the stage, put on my headphones, and began playing. I recorded this session about three times so that I would have a good recording.

I went back to the booth and listened to what I had just played. While I was listening to the song, I saw a vision of my little girl dancing in one of her dresses to the song. Needless to say, I just sat there and wept like a baby.

Our violinist Carolyn came in, saw me crying, and asked what was wrong. I told her that I had just written a new song. So I played it for her. While she listened, I shared with her what I had been seeing. When the song was finished, she looked at me and said, "That's beautiful, Brian. I could see Victoria dancing. You should call it 'The Dance.'"

Wow! Thank You, God. But that song was never recorded on our Daystar CDs. In fact I rarely played the song in church or anywhere. This song will reappear later.

In 2005 the Lord would surprise me again. Right after a Sunday morning service at Grace UMC in Katy, Tx, the Lord gave me another song. I played through it three times. Thinking *I got this*, I then sat down. Church began, the worship team came in, and we played the morning service. Pastor Jim brought the message.

I was to play after he finished speaking and also play during the prayer and altar time. While the pastor was wrapping up his sermon, I started thinking about the song. *Yikes!* I had forgotten what I played earlier. I could not even remember what I did or how the song went!

Not to panic. I could play something else. But I really felt that since the Lord gave this to me, that this was meant to be played *now*. Yes, I was panicked! It was now time to go up to the stage.

As I walked up to the stage I was praying, *Lord, please, bring this song back to my memory! Only you can give this to me now.*

How cool is God? I sat down at my keyboard. The church used a headphone monitor system for the musicians to hear their music. As I sat down, I placed my headphones on my head. When I did...*surprise!* The song was in my head and ready to go. I just started playing. It may not seem like it to you, but this was a step of faith for me. It is so simple but hard learning to trust Him in *all* things.

Okay, Brian, what happened to this music? Hang on— we're almost there.

While we were visiting Christian Faith Church in 2009, Leah and I had a couple of words spoken over us from Brother Alfred, a visiting evangelist from India. He shared that this was the time, that God was going to set us on a new journey, and that this place would be our new location. Both of these were confirmation to our prayers.

One of these words given was that I would move more into a prophetic music ministry. This would be a sign of another step in faith for me. What did this look like? What would I be doing? How would I do a prophetic music ministry? Is this something that the band would be doing? All good questions!

There was a great outpouring of the Holy Spirit at that church that would extend for three days. Many people were prayed for, new visions revealed, and hearts and lives were changed.

On that Sunday night Leah and I headed back to the church. I felt a prompting from the Holy Spirit to ask Amy, the worship leader, if I could play keyboards with the praise team. She said it would be okay. She was the main keyboard player for the praise team and I was in a supporting role that evening.

It was a great worship set. The praise and worship started at 6:00 p.m. and went until 6:40 p.m., then Brother Alfred took to the stage to bring the message.

All of the musicians were walking off the stage. As I got ready to go, Brother Alfred looked at me, and in his Indian accent said "*Baroththter Brian* (my italics here), would you please stay and play for awhile?"

I replied, "Sure."

I figured that I would play for about five to ten minutes. Then like other pastors, he would turn to me and say, "Thank you, that will be all for now."

As I sat down and began to play, Brother Alfred began to give a powerful word to the church, and then suddenly he started to walk out into the congregation.

He would look around for a few seconds, and then would call someone to come up to the altar. He would then speak a word of prophecy over them when he had a word from God to share. To see the person's face and demeanor change—it was as if God was right there revealing secrets, ambitions, passions, and pains that only that person would know about.

It was incredible—breathtaking. As I sat there playing quietly in the background, I was in awe. I did not really pay too much attention to what I was playing other than just letting the Holy Spirit guide me through the music.

Suddenly, I had a pain in my back. I was slumped over almost on the keyboard. Then I would get a cramp in my leg. I would have to stand up—still playing and stretching—then sit back down.

I thought, *Oh my, how I wish that I brought my keyboard bench to sit on. It is far more comfortable than this hard plastic stool.* But I continued playing. Lauren, from the praise team, would come up and bring me water.

Brother Alfred continued walking out into the congregation and bringing people back up to the altar to speak a word over them. Suddenly, he was asking Leah to come. I smiled. I knew that God would have something powerful to share for her. When she got to the front of the church, he asked her, "Your husband—is he here?"

She pointed over his shoulder and said, "Yes. He is playing the keyboard." Brother Alfred said, "Oh, yes, yes.

Brian, you can stop now. Would you please come down here with your wife?"

At this point that I looked up at the clock. It was 11:25 p.m.! My, oh my! Had I been there since 6 p.m., playing?

This would be just one of the many times I would get the opportunity to play along with the worship team and play the keyboard during times of prayer at the altar.

A woman named Cindy handled all of the recordings from the services at church. Leah and I had requested some copies so that we could go back through and listen to the places where Brother Alfred had spoken to us.

A couple of months later, Cindy stopped me in church and said, "I really enjoyed listening to your keyboard music. It was incredible. It was powerful and anointed. It's too bad that we couldn't separate your playing and Brother Alfred speaking. You really need to get this recorded and put it on a CD with your other music that you play from the altar."

During the next year, I would hear this from some of the other people who were at the church and had listened to the CD. They would ask me, "Do you have any of *your* music on CD?"

Sometime later, *much* later, Leah and I were looking through and listening to some of the CDs from the service. We had just finished listening to the part where Alfred had spoken to us. We looked at one another—wow! That was powerful! Listening some more, Leah then said, "Briny,

I think you need to work on this music and think about doing a solo keyboard CD."

Listening to some more music, Leah and I just wept: the music was beautiful. For you musicians, this is the type of music that was just being played from the heart or in the spirit— a free-for-all.

We continued listening to CDs. When we got to disc 3, something mysterious and strange happened before my ears.

Brother Alfred was speaking a word to someone in the congregation. I was playing the keyboard. Suddenly, there was a long hiss and crackling noise in the recording!

Alfred's microphone has gone off. He is nowhere to be heard on the CD. All that you can hear for the next twelve minutes on the disc is just Brian playing the keyboard— playing in the Spirit!

This was not anything that I had ever written, composed, or worked on. Nothing! Nada! Zip! This was just Brian, playing for the Lord, and His music flowing through me. All in all, it turned out that there would be twenty minutes of music.

I was not able to rerecord anything or play over the songs because of the live recording. After much prayer, Leah and I and a few others felt that the Lord wanted this to be on a project "as is." It was His live music, playing in the Spirit. I was merely a vessel to be used by Him.

In July the following year, 2010, our dear friends Gary and Cindy Hitchcock, along with their two children Eli and Keely came out to The Hill for a couple days' visit. It was an awesome time of fellowship. We listened to music and cooked Foutz Fried Chicken. We had green beans and tomatoes that I grew in our neighbor's field. Their family even pulled some watermelons that I was growing. They were huge!

While there, Gary and I listened to music I had recorded, and then listened to some CDs from the time when Brother Alfred was here in October 2009.

Gary was listening to the CD, then something incredible happened. As I played for Gary the part where the microphone went out and it was just me playing, he said, "Wow…do you know what this is?"

Puzzled, I said, "No, what is it?"

Gary looked at me with tears in his eyes and said, "That is you. That is you playing your story."

Surprised, I looked straight back in his face and replied, "My story? What do you mean, my story?"

Gary shared that I was playing from my heart—in the Spirit. I was playing for Him and I was sharing my story, my walk in life. *Wow*! How powerful was that! He then said, "Brian, you have got to get this on a recording along with some of the other music that you have written. This is amazing! The music is anointed, and it is music that will bring healing."

After they left, Leah and I prayed about the CD, and then we got a confirmation. It was time to get this keyboard music recorded. I recorded several altar songs that the Lord had given me over the last year.

A month later, on a Saturday morning, Leah got up with me and we headed into Houston to meet with Joey Garza at Full Measure Productions. I seemed to be relaxed, but I was really praying that we would be able to use those items that I already recorded on my digital recorder at the house.

When we got to the studio, Leah anointed all of our hands and her throat with oil and we prayed over the CD project and recording. My prayer was, "Oh Lord, let us be able to use most of the recorded items. Let Joey be able to use the songs recorded live at CFC and the song from Grace UMC called 'Heavenly Flight,' as well as 'The Dance.'"

Wow! What a session! The recorded tracks transferred easily and Joey did his magical work. We did not want to lose the anointing on CFC songs. God was all over this music. So, Joey fixed the finger mistakes and pulled everything together for a great recording. We did record "Don's Song," but re-titled it "Dawn's Song." Joey is *awesome*! God is amazing!

With everything done, there was only one song left to record: "Breath of God." I was concerned about this song because I usually just played this freestyle with no tempo. But listening to the song, it did not feel right. So Joey found a soft click track to use for the tempo to record.

As I began to play, I felt the Lord's presence on me, in me, around me. Halfway through the song I was weeping—I was afraid that I would not be able to finish the song. After we were through recording the song, I shared that I felt like I had been seated at the foot of the throne of God and that I had been playing for Him! Truly, it was for an Audience of One!

This would begin my very first solo keyboard project. This is a step that I would have never taken on my own. It seems in life that we always want to be in charge of our destiny because we are told by others that is how you succeed. But to give up control and to let God direct your life, you have to be willing to give up that drive and let Him guide you. This does not mean that you give up and just sit back. It means that you give everything to Him, let Him reveal the vision for your life, and then let Him guide you through the process toward the realization of the vision for your purpose in life.

They say that luck is being prepared when opportunity arrives. I believe the key in life is being prepared, open, willing, and obedient to be used by God. I am reminded of what Smith Wigglesworth once said:

> As soon as Paul saw the light from heaven above the brightness of the sun, he said, "Lord, what wilt thou have me to do?" (Acts 9:6)
>
> And as soon as he was willing to yield he was in a condition where God could meet his need; where

God could display His power; where God could have the man. Oh, beloved, are you saying today, "What wilt thou have me to do?" The place of yieldedness is just where God wants us.

Who knows best what you are really capable of, other than God? You must learn to trust Him. You have to be willing to take that first step—that step of faith.

Thanks for the Break!

Leah

> And we know that God causes all things to work together for good to those who love God, to those who are called according to His purpose.
>
> —Romans 8:28 (NASB)

Sometimes, we simply get *too* busy! We are running here and there, working, doing other things, visiting people, and we may forget to slow down and pay attention to things that are all around us. Sometimes we simply need be still. It is so easy to fill our days with "busyness." However, we should stop and take time to spend with the Lord—either with prayers, praises, or just being still in His Presence!

I remember that, once upon a time, I was really busy with "stuff." We were running here and there: I was working for a friend in Katy, Brian and I were visiting different churches in our area in the hopes that we could come there to speak. Even the large grocery store is more than thirty minutes away from our home!

I think that the Lord wanted me to be more focused on Him. This was accomplished in a rather bizarre manner. Here's the story of what happened:

On Sunday morning, the day after Christmas 2010, Brian left early for a church in a nearby town so that he could rehearse with their praise team. I drove myself in later to join him for the service.

When the service was over, Brian stayed behind to assist in getting the equipment stored away, and helping members of the praise team with packing up their instruments. We then went to lunch in Brenham with our good friends Don and Lee Ann.

After lunch, I drove on home. I stopped at a store and got a drink with ice and headed to The Hill. Brian would be home later. When I got back to the house I started to walk up the stairs to our bedroom in order to change clothes before I settled in to watch a football playoff game. Just a note in passing: the NY Giants played the Packers and got *stomped* (45 to 17)!

As I began my ascent, all of a sudden my right ankle gave way and I fell down. I was embarrassed about falling but managed to get back up quickly. I had dropped my drink, spilling my drink and ice all over the floor. I managed to get to the kitchen and grabbed a towel to wipe it up. My right ankle was really hurting. When I got back to the mess, I was not able to clean it up. I knew that Brian would see this and clean it up for me once he learned that I had fallen. I felt that my ankle may have been sprained, so I grabbed an ice pack and headed toward the stairs. Our bedroom was *upstairs*. Ugh!

But before heading upstairs, I hobbled over to the downstairs bathroom. I remembered that I had sprained my left foot about ten years earlier and needed to have a pair of crutches. As it turned out, it was cheaper to buy them than to rent them. I found the crutches and painfully walked slowly up the steps to the bedroom where I changed clothes and got into the bed.

A short time later, Brian got home. When he walked into the hall by the stairs, he saw the spilled drink still on the floor and called out, "Hey! Where are you?"

"I'm upstairs," I replied.

Brian then hollered back, "Hey! Why is there ice on the floor and a towel covering the ice?"

"I tripped and fell, spilling my drink. I'm sorry I didn't go back down to clean it up."

Brian sighed, "Okay…I'll clean it up." Brian cleaned up the mess, and then came up to check on me.

When Brian came up, he saw me lying in bed. Then he saw the crutches and stared at them. I shared that I may have twisted my ankle when I fell because it really hurt a lot and was beginning to swell up. He then touched around my ankle to see how bad it was.

"*Ouch!* That hurts!" I replied.

He said we would call for an appointment the next morning so that the doctor could check it out and perhaps lend us an ankle wrap while it healed.

The next day we were able to get an appointment for that morning in Katy, Texas. By this time, the ankle was swollen a whole lot and had turned purple from the bruising. Also, it hurt *a lot more*! I shared with Brian that this hurt more than any other time I had hurt my ankle! It was swollen *and* painful!

We arrived at the doctor's office and got checked in. We waited for a short time, then the doctor came into the room. We already knew the doctor, so we exchanged hellos and Merry Christmas with him.

I explained what had happened the day before. He looked at and felt my ankle, and decided to have an X-ray made. The clinic had an X-ray facility right next door, so I hobbled over on my crutches. The X-rays were done immediately. I hobbled back to the doctor's office, returned to the doctor's exam room and waited for the results.

The doctor came in shortly and put the results on a TV monitor that was in the exam room. Sure enough, all of us could see clearly that there *was* a break on the ankle bone. *Ugh!*

We were then referred to a specialist who was a surgeon so that he could look at the ankle. We called his office. They said that he did not usually come in on Mondays and was not planning on coming in that day, but that they would call and see what he wanted us to do.

The doctor had written me a prescription for pain, so Brian and I decided to go get the medication filled and wait for the other doctor (it's not like we had anything *else* to do—ha!). We prayed that the doctor would call back soon, otherwise we were going to have to go home and just wait for his call.

After waiting an hour, we got a phone call from the nurse in the specialist's office. She said that the doctor actually *did* come in to the office. He had called our doctor and said for us to get in there as soon as possible! Praise God!

We got in to see the doctor almost immediately that afternoon. After reviewing the X-rays, the doctor said that they could not do anything right now because of the swelling but that I would need a cast put on my leg to immobilize the ankle. Once again, I hobbled back to the other room to have the cast done. What a hassle! I'd also need to be off the leg for the next ten to twelve *weeks*. Yikes!

Well, to make a long story short, the male nurse preparing the cast gave me several options as to the color of the cast. I selected a pretty baby blue. When the cast was done, I was rolled out to our truck in a wheelchair, and home we went.

Now, remember that we live out in the country in a large house that is really up off the ground. In other words, there were *stairs* from the ground to the porch. *Ugh!* I gingerly hobbled up the five or six steps to get to the back door and enter. Brian helped me as much as he could and got me settled in on our couch downstairs.

I did not want to be downstairs, but I was told *not* to go upstairs. This meant that I could not sleep in my own bed!

Brian was truly my hero over the next twelve weeks since I could not go up the stairs and spent all my days (and nights) on that couch. It was pretty boring downstairs with no TV to watch, but I could read...and read I did! He also got me a couple of crossword puzzle books to work in, so I was all set.

Brian asked me if there was anything I needed. Thinking about this, I said, "You know, my computer work area is upstairs in the hallway. Is there any way you could bring my computer down here so that I could check my emails and get online?"

"Sure!" he said. "I'll get right on it for you—anything for my bride." Then my hero moved my computer system downstairs and got me all set up. What a guy!

In the meantime I read and listened to music. Brian had recently released his first solo keyboard CD called "Reflections," and that became my musical "medication" while I lived downstairs on that couch. I listened to it over, and over, and over! It truly was calming for me during those long days and nights.

The next visit to the doctor came. Again he spoke of putting pins and screws in my ankle. Yikes! I quickly asked if he would simply wrap it up when the cast came off, and see if it might heal okay without a cast. The doctor was very skeptical but did as I asked. The cast was removed and we discussed what else needed to be done.

Very reluctantly, the doctor agreed—although he wasn't sure it would work. We made a deal. He said he would give me a couple more weeks to see if it was healing, but if not to his liking, he would have to put in the screws.

Now all this time, Brian and I had been praying for the Lord to touch that ankle and mend it completely. If that meant to let the doctor operate and put in screws, I would accept it, but I just felt that God was a God who heals, and I wanted to take Him at His word! I truly believed that God *was* able to heal that broken ankle.

Basically, I told the doctor that I wanted to wait and see what God would do. I know he was very skeptical. However, he said he'd let me do it my way until my next visit—I think it was in three or four weeks—but after that he would have to operate. I agreed, and we left for home after the ankle was rewrapped.

> O Lord my God, I cried to You and You have healed me. (Ps. 30:2, NASB)

I took comfort from this scripture, and it gave me that little "boost of faith" that I needed to stand firm. But then, when I looked this passage up in The Message translation, my spirit leapt inside me!

> God, my God, I yelled for help and you put me together. God, you pulled me out of the grave, gave me another chance at life when I was down-and-out. (Ps. 30:2–3, MSG)

When we got back home, I began to play music on the stereo next to "my bed" (the couch) constantly, literally around the clock. The music from Brian's CD was played over and over. Brian could hear me playing it downstairs, even during the night. He later told me that he got *really* tired listening to that music—even if it *was* his!

About two weeks later, as I lay on the couch one night, I prayed once again for God to heal that ankle. All of a sudden my ankle, as well as my entire leg, felt like it was *on fire*! I prayed for the pain to stop, or that this was God's healing! Finally, the pain subsided and I was able to sleep. I told Brian about this the next morning, and we prayed that God had touched that ankle to heal it completely.

A few days later we drove in for our next visit to the doctor. We arrived at the office and were sent back to have more X-rays. Like we did before, once the X-rays were done, we waited for the doctor to come in.

When he entered the room, the doctor looked a little perplexed. He shook his head over and over, then made the comment, "Well, I don't understand it! Call it karma, or luck, or prayer—that ankle is *completely* healed!"

Woo-hoo! I looked at the doctor and said, "I'll take *prayer*, thank you very much!"

He just kept looking at me, shaking his head. Then he said that it was okay for me remove the bandage and to be careful.

As I reflected on this step of faith, I realized that because my ankle was broken and I was forced to be still, God used that time to help me to grow in *Him*. Because I prayed for healing and believed that He was *able* to do it, He blessed me with exactly what I had asked for!

Looking back at what happened during my trial with my broken ankle, I realize that my faith grew so much during that time. It was partly because I was fairly isolated downstairs on the couch, but also I was spending much time in His Presence, praying and praising Him for the healing I had asked for! This was truly a *mighty* step of faith for both Brian and me. We took a giant step of faith and God honored it. All I can do is to *praise him!*

> See now that I, I am He, and there is no god besides Me; It is I who put to death and give life. I have wounded, and it is I who heal and there is no one who can deliver from My hand. (Deut. 32:39, NASB)

The Adoption

Brian and Leah

> But Jesus called the children to him and said, "Let the little children come to me, and do not hinder them, for the kingdom of God belongs to such as these."
>
> —Luke 18:16 (NIV)

In March 2010, after moving to the country, we had some dear friends from Katy, Jim, and Marlene come up for a weekend visit to our home on The Hill.

Joining them for the weekend trip were their three foster children: Lora, Jackie, and Krystle. All three of the girls were around the age of 12–14. The three girls had been placed in foster care due to family challenges. The two youngest girls, Lora and Jackie were sisters and had been fostered by Jim and Marlene for some time. Krystle had recently come to them, and was still learning to be part of their family. Prior to their visit, Marlene had shared with us that Krystle had been a challenge to Jim, herself, and the two girls.

Marlene felt that a drive in the country and time away from the city would give them all a chance to unwind and just be themselves. We learned that the two sisters had previously asked Jesus into their hearts but that Krystle had not and was not interested.

We were so happy to have them out to visit but kept a close eye on Krystle, watching her interaction with her new foster "family."

Leah noticed that she seemed to be craving special attention, and when she did not get it, she would do something that was wrong, just so she'd get the attention she obviously craved.

Leah shared with me that she felt that Krystle's birth family may have not paid attention to her, causing her to act out and get *some* kind of attention even it was negative and hurtful to her.

Leah prayed in her spirit for something that might help in this situation, and hopefully let Marlene and Jim and the other girls have a break from so much drama.

The three girls really enjoyed walking around the property, strolling down the long dirt road in front of the house, going down to the pond in the next field, and picking spring flowers for Leah.

We had a nice time together, visiting and fixing lunch. It was great to see how much fun they were having… without a single television set, video, or computer game to entertain them.

They were actually having *fun* just being young girls!

When lunch was ready, we all sat down and had a great meal together. Each girl could hardly wait to tell us what they liked the best about their visit so far. Lots of laughing and enjoyment during lunch, as well as some *great* home-cooked Foutz fried chicken!

Later, we all moved into the living room; just talking and relaxing. The girls shared how much fun they were having in the country.

Then we asked the girls a question.

"What do you really want in your life?"

To our surprise, as they began to share what they wanted, each one wanted to be adopted. They wanted to have loving parents, and they shared where they wanted to live.

Lora shared that she wanted to be adopted by a family that lived in the city. She just loved the city and all the neat things that she could do. You know…like go to the movies, to the mall, etc.

Jackie, her biological sister wanted to be adopted, but wanted to live in country. She wanted to be around the open fields, trees, horses, cows, and other animals. She liked the smell of the country and really felt alive here.

Now Krystle had been in the foster care system for some time and was no relation to the other girls. She wore a baseball cap over her long blonde hair. It was a "tough guy" look for her. Independence was her strong suit as they say. She hardly ever took it off except for when she went to bed.

She really liked being out here on The Hill, and felt that she wanted to live in the country.

Then I asked her, "So, you would like to be adopted and live out in the country in a place like this?" Her response was surprising to all of us. "I think so, but I am not sure…"

When we asked her why, she said, "What happens if they adopt me, end up not liking me, and decide they don't want me anymore?"

She felt if someone decided that they did not want her, they might just send her back.

I felt a prompting in my spirit when she shared this. Then, the Lord began to work.

I asked all of the girls, "Do you know what it means to be adopted?"

They looked around at each other and said, "I don't know."

I began to share a story from Old Testament times how a Jewish family lived. I told them that the father of the house could divorce his wife and that he could disown his own children. He also could give them nothing during his lifetime or leave them anything after death.

It was also a common practice that if a relative of this man died and left children, then he could adopt the children from that family and they would become his children.

Jewish law specified that when that happened the father could never, never disown those children or disinherit them from the family. It was forbidden under the law for him to give them away or disown them.

I then began to share about God's promise to us—that we are His adopted children, and that we can never be disowned or left behind. And, *that* is what it means when we accept Jesus as our personal Saviour.

> For you have not received a spirit of slavery leading to fear again, but you have received a spirit of adoption as sons by which we cry out, Abba father! (Rom. 8:15, NASB)

Now here is something really interesting:

> He predestined us for adoption as sons through Jesus Christ, according to the purpose of His will. (Eph. 1:5, ESV)

When I finished the story, I looked at Krystle and said, "Would you like to be adopted by our Lord and King?"

Krystle looked at me, lowered her head, and quietly said, "Yes."

When she said "yes," I looked at Leah, and then Leah said to Krystle, "Why don't you come over here and sit by me."

Krystle got up off of the floor and sat down next to Leah.

Leah gently picked up her hand and held it closely then said, "Would you like to invite Jesus into your life?"

Krystle reached up and took off her hat. Then she laid her cap on her lap and looked at Leah and gently replied, "Yes…I do!"

I like the way that Leah tells the story from here:

"As we visited, I began to talk with Krystle about Jesus. I asked her if she had ever been to church, and she said not before she came to live with Marlene and Jim. Her family did not even talk about Jesus, much less know Him.

"I shared with her that Jesus had come to earth a long time ago. Just like us, He was born as a baby, grew up, and became a man. However, the difference between His life and ours was that *He* is the Son of God! Because of Who Jesus is, He chose to come to earth, be born as a baby, grow up, and then share with other people Who He was. That they could be certain that, when their life here was over, they would spend eternity in heaven with Him.

"I explained that God had sent Jesus to earth to let all people know that *God loves them*, and that they can have a place in heaven with God when they die, if they were willing to believe that Jesus is God's Son. That if they would simply ask Jesus to live within their hearts, they too would be with God in heaven one day!

"As I spoke, I noticed that Krystal was listening very intently to every word. She was shocked that Jesus was killed by the people of that time and that they had treated Him so very badly.

"I didn't go into a lot of details, but she realized that He had suffered very much. When I told her about Him being put into a grave, she looked so sad. I know that she must have thought, *Well, that's it then...Jesus was killed and buried.*

"I will never forget her face when I then told her that three days later, Jesus actually rose from the dead, left that grave, and then went back to heaven to live there with the Father God!

"Her face lit up at that! I told her that because of what Jesus did, *all* of us can have the opportunity to go to heaven and be with God and Jesus. Krystal looked at me and asked me, 'How?'

"I was so happy to tell her that if she believed that Jesus Christ died for her and her sins, and if she wanted Him to live inside her heart, all she needed to do was to ask Him in. She said she really wanted to do that, so I held her hand and we prayed a short prayer—me first, then Krystal. Her prayer was so sweet, as she asked Jesus to live in her heart.

"When we were finished, I told the others that Krystal had something to share with everyone. When they were looking at her, she sweetly told them that she had Jesus in her heart now.

"The other two girls rushed to hug her, knowing that they too had asked Jesus into their hearts before this day. Marlene and Jim were also very happy to see Krystal make this decision. There were hugs all around. What a wonderful way to end a great day in the country!"

What an amazing example of a step of faith—stepping out in faith to become one of His. Glory to God!

Now here is something interesting to share with others… and it is a great promise to those who feel abandoned by their parents.

> Although my father and my mother have forsaken me, yet the Lord will take me up, adopt me as His child. (Ps 27:10, AMP)

Wow! What a comfort to know that ALL who come to Him will be adopted as His own child!

More Than Enough

Brian

> You will make known to me the path of life; in your presence is fullness of joy; in your right hand there are pleasures forever.
>
> —Psalm 16:11 (NASB)

Leah and I have found over these past years that if you want to do something, go and ask the Father.

No, I don't mean convince yourself that what you want to do is a great idea, and then we ask the Father to bless it.

We are all guilty of doing that—"we" decide what "we" want to do in life. It doesn't matter whether it is taking a trip, going on a vacation, borrowing money, changing jobs, or purchasing something. Most of us have the tendency to use our brain, and then calculate the odds, and then decide on the best option for us. Then—wait for it—we ask God (or tell God) to *bless it*!

Wow! I can look back at my life and see where I too did just exactly that. I made the decision. I said I would pray about it, but I didn't really pray. Based upon how I "felt," I then made the decision to do whatever it was that I wanted to do. At the end I tacked on, "Oh and yeah, and God… please bless this endeavor. Amen!"

Later, when things don't quite work out the way we wanted them to, we—using our brain—start questioning God about *our* combined decision. Ha! As a TV host once said, "How's that working out for you?"

After we moved to the country, the Lord provided a nice "little" house on a hill. We gave a new name to this wonderful new place: "The Hill."

As we began to move more and more into full time ministry, we found that it was less stressful to be "led by the Spirit, rather than the soul." And yes, that took some time for us to get used to doing. It's a process, as they say.

> Your word is lamp unto my feet and a light to my path. (Ps. 119:105, NASB)

Leah and I had finished writing our first book in 2010, *From Misery to Ministry—A Walk of Faith through the Loss of a Loved One.* With final editing done, we began looking for the right publisher.

We began asking Him for permission and direction on getting the book published.

We literally spent the next three months reviewing publishers and trying to learn the pros and cons of publishing. For those of you who have written a book or a journal of some kind, you start looking at publishing companies. There are big companies and small companies. There is also self-publishing and on-demand publishing. The list of choices is pretty long. Your head begins to spin at some point. But, in the end the Lord directed us to Tate Publishing in Mustang, OK. They are a fine Christian publisher and we have been on an incredible journey with them ever since. God is good.

During the final process, and as the book was being published, the publisher reminded us that there would be an audiobook. Wow! How cool is that?

It was now mid-July of 2011. We were already out doing book signings and asking the Lord what to do next. It was at this point that Leah and I began to chat about the audiobook. We began asking ourselves, "I wonder if they will let us read for the audio book? Hmmm...I wonder if they would let us record *our* voices to use for the audiobook?"

So, we fired off an email to Tate Publishing. We asked them if we could read for the audiobook, and what the process was. They replied by email and said that they usually do not have authors read for the audio book and they usually use professional speakers.

Curious, we wrote back, "Could *we* read for the book?" We then got a phone call with their reply. The person working in that area said, "We will consider this request only if you and your wife submit one chapter each as a test. You will need to have the recording professionally recorded and mastered. When you finish, send the final mastered copy to us for review." With that I replied, "Thank you!"

After the call, Leah and I discussed this some more and prayed. We felt led to get more information and decided to call our friend Joey Garza.

Joey had recorded an album for us with our Christian music group The Daystar Project, and he owns Full Measure Sound in Houston. He is also a close friend of ours.

We shared with him about this new opportunity. He was excited for us, and said he would love to help us. Leah and I said to each other, "Let's at least see if this is a possibility."

Leah and I recorded our voices at home on a digital recorder that I had, and sent the WAV (voice) files to Joey. He then mastered the recording for us. We sent off the final mastered CD to Tate.

Okay, about now you are asking yourself, "Hey! What about this thing of going to the Father? Where is that in this story?"

Hang on, it's coming.

About a week later, we got the news that they would let us read for the audiobook. Yea! But—here it comes—we would have to go to Oklahoma at our own expense to read for the book. No stipend, no help with finances or a place to stay—literally *all* on our own dime!

Like most people, we really did not have the extra money to go. If we did go, we would be using money needed for regular expenses, meaning within the next three or four weeks we would be short of money to pay our bills. Then what would we do?

Yes, there are people who would have done anything and sacrificed everything to go. You know put it on a credit card and pay for it later. A lot of people, caught in the emotion of the moment, would have said, "Let's git 'er done!"

But when we moved up here to the country, one of the first words spoken over us prior to our move was this: "Do not buy or build, and stay debt free, so that if and when the Lord needs to move you, you will have no excuses and you can move on a moment's notice!"

So far, we had been faithful in that area. Now what were we to do?

This is when we began to put our faith into action. The Lord had provided everything that we needed before. This included the right time in the selling of our home, the new location where He wanted us to be, and the home on The Hill.

Leah and I prayed and felt the prompting of the Holy Spirit. At the end of our praying, here is how we responded.

We asked the Lord for His permission to go to Oklahoma and to record for the audiobook. Yes, it was like going to your dad and saying, "Father…can I have your permission to go the ball game or movie?" Sounds kind of corny, but this is exactly what we did.

We placed our request at the foot of the altar. We then felt led to send an email out to our prayer intercessors on our ministry prayer team. Here was our prayer request:

> We have been given an opportunity to go to Tate Publishing in Oklahoma and read the chapters from our book for an audio recording.
>
> We are asking you, our prayer partners, to be in agreement with us to ask the Lord for His permission to go.
>
> Should the Father give us His permission, we have calculated the cost for this trip to be $800.00. This will cover the gas to and from Oklahoma using our Dodge Durango. It will also cover the cost of meals and lodging for two days. So we are also asking that should He give us permission to go, that He would provide the funds to make the trip possible.

Leah and I were in agreement ourselves, that if we did not get His permission, we would not go. And He had to provide for *all* of the provisions. No excuses.

I want to share with you that we did not send out the request to a large list of people, nor did it go to people that we knew would have disposable income to support us. This only went to our prayer intercessors. We only asked that the Father give us permission and that He would be the one to provide for us.

My wife Leah has a great saying: "When the Lord is the one doing the providing, He will give you exactly what you need." Then, when the Father answers the prayers of His children, she says, "I am no longer surprised… only delighted!"

One of the many promises of His word is found in the book of Mark.

> Therefore I tell you, whatever you ask for in prayer, believe that you have received it, and it will be yours. (Mark 11:24, NIV)

About ten days after our request was sent out, Leah and I were in a Wednesday night Bible study that was meeting at our church. At the end of the study, we said our goodbyes to people, and we were heading out the door. Suddenly, our pastor came up to us and stopped us. He said, "The Lord wanted me to tell you to pack your bags!"

I looked at him and said, "It looks like the Lord has answered our prayers, thank you!"

Okay, we had gotten an affirmation and it now looked like we were going. But I was not too excited yet—you know, I am a guy! I was still waiting for the provision. (This is part of the faith walk: believing that you will receive).

Leah and I discussed this the next day on one of our country drives. We were still in agreement about our prayer request. If the Father gave us permission, then He would have to provide the resources.

This is where it really starts to get interesting. The following Tuesday, Leah and I were on our way back from Northwest Houston, passing through Hempstead, then on to Brenham to see a storeowner about a book signing. We stopped in Hempstead briefly to visit some friends of ours.

While standing outside their home, we shared with them our prayer request. They really wanted to help us. But we let them know that we were not looking for anything but only asking them to be in agreement with us on this prayer request. We then prayed together, and Leah and I left.

Now this particular friend was someone who I had known through our old music ministry. Usually she and I would exchange an email and or phone call, but never did she call Leah.

As we were leaving the town of Hempstead, she called Leah on her mobile phone—not me! This was kind of strange; I did not even know that she had Leah's phone number. Leah answered her phone and I heard, "Where are you?" Leah told her that we were about two miles down the road. She then told Leah, "Turn around *right now* and come back—we want to talk to you!"

So we returned to their home. When we got out of the truck, the couple came over to us and shared this, "After you left, we felt a prompting in our spirit that when asking God for anything He will provide whatever you need. We want to follow through with what the Holy Spirit told us to do." With that they handed me something and pressed it in the palm of my hand. I placed the item in my shirt pocket. Then we prayed together and left.

When we were on the road again, Leah reached over and took whatever it was out of my shirt pocket. She said, "Do you know what this is?"

"No," I replied.

She looked again at the paper in her hand and then said, "You really don't know what this is?"

"No, I have not looked at anything."

Leah said, "Do you know how much this is?" I looked over at her and smiled. Then these words came out of my mouth, "Yes, it's an eighth of the trip."

Yes, that is exactly what it was. I had no idea, but in a way I knew what it was. I could feel it in my spirit.

Wow! Go, God! But wait…there's more!

Two days later another set of friends in Katy had us over for dinner.

They shared a story of a recent Bible study that they had done with some coworkers. They shared some of the neat things they had learned and then a strange story about one of the CD discs. They said that one day the CD did not work. They tried it in all of the computers and DVD players in the office.

So they went ahead and played the next disc in the set. This happened for a couple of weeks in a row. Leah and I looked at each other. We were confused, but listened. At first we did not understand what was going on, then they shared this.

Their final CD had Jesus talking about a particular story. It had to do with "the least of these." Everyone in the study thought the "least of these" were the widows and orphans, but it turned out that it had to do with those people who on the frontline in ministry.

So, they asked themselves, who do we know who is on the frontline in ministry? To our surprise they both said, "Brian and Leah!"

With that, the husband handed me a folded paper and said that they wanted to sow a seed in what we were doing.

In some ways, this blessing was different from the first, but in other ways it was as if the first blessing was being repeated. On the way home, Leah and I had the same conversation. After reaching into my shirt pocket, she said, "Do you know what this is?"

"No."

"Do you know how much this is?"

With a smile, I replied, "Yes…it's an eighth of the trip!"

When Sunday rolled around, we were back in church, and one of the church members walked past me and dropped a folded check in my lap. I looked at her and said, "Do you want me to put this in the offering plate for you?"

Her reply came fast, "No…it's for your trip!"

Wow! Go, God!

With only two weeks to go, Leah and I were still in agreement, believing that the Lord was going to provide for the trip. We did not know how, but His word says He will.

Then another friend of ours called. She had been very helpful to us when Victoria had died. She had given our names to a number of different people who had lost children over the years, and we would go and minister to them.

She knew of our prayer request. After some discussion, she asked me how much we still needed.

Now, this is where it gets really interesting—not just for now, but for what will happen later. We had $250.00. I told her that we were close and that we still needed about $500.00. I don't know why I said this, but it just fell out of my mouth.

She said that they wanted to bless us and the check was on the way. Once again, God was at work.

It was now about eight days from leaving for Oklahoma. God, you are so good. We have just about all that we had prayed for.

This was where God really shows up and fulfills His promise.

A close and dear friend of ours called me and shared that he had just recently come into some additional money. He said that after praying and talking with his wife, they had decided to sow a seed into our ministry.

He said, "Brother Brian, how much do you still need for the trip?"

Okay, this is the point that, as a guy, you want to say, "Hey! We are close enough! We're good. We got what we need."

You know, $ 750.00 is close enough. Ha!

But the Lord *stopped* me in my tracks and kept my mouth closed.

It is like I heard this voice say, "He has asked you a specific question…you need to give him a specific response."

With that, I replied, "Well, actually, to tell you the truth my brother, we are about $50 shy of the original amount of money needed for the trip." (I just stopped and did not say another word).

His loving response startled me. "Brother Brian, do you believe that the Lord will give you exactly what you need?"

"Yes," I said.

Again he spoke. "Do you also believe that the Lord can give you more than enough so that He can provide for *all* things?"

Again I replied, "Yes, I believe that He can do that. He can do all things!"

To which came this reply, "Brother Brian, we are going to send you a check for $500.00 because the Lord wants you to have more than enough to make this trip!"

At this point, I am choked up. There are tears running down my face. All that I can say is, "Thank you, Jesus! Thank you—thank you, Jesus!"

Yes, Lord, yes!

When you are learning to take those steps of faith—whether they are giant steps or just baby steps—the Lord our God will provide for *all* things. And it is these *steps of faith* that move us closer and closer to being in His will—to be used by Him, for Him, and to further His Kingdom.

I am reminded when David called out to the Lord:

> I have called upon You, for You will answer me, O God; Incline Your ear to me, hear my speech. (Ps. 17: 6, NASB)

We packed our bags and off to Oklahoma we went. Why? Because of His promise, for He is faithful and true!

Leah and I had a wonderful and fun drive up and back; and yes, we read for the audio book!

It was the 12th of September 2011. We arrived in Oklahoma City, early on a Monday afternoon. Another blessing had been given to us. The Lord provided a place for us to stay with my cousin Sherri in Oklahoma City. Two wonderful nights and a dinner with her and her husband the first night. Then on the second night, we were blessed with a dinner with my close musician friend Randy and his wife. Wow! We were not prepared for this!

God is full of surprises and blessings!

On Tuesday morning, we headed to Mustang, Oklahoma to Tate Publishing. When we arrived, we were greeted by a nice young woman named Shauna. We went inside and almost immediately we began recording. Leah and I were literally in the booth, recording all day.

We had a couple breaks, then lunch, and continued recording until the office closed. We came back early at

7:00 a.m. on Wednesday morning. With the Lord's help, we were able to finish the recording around 9:30 a.m.

After completing the recording project, Shauna gave us a tour of the office. We got to meet the design people for the book, the staff who worked on the video trailer, and the rest of the crew who worked on the manuscript. Wow—it was like ten people who all had a hand in bringing our book to life!

Afterward, Shauna took us over the main office to meet our marketing representative, Jim Miller and the rest of the marketing team.

God had truly blessed us with a great team and support staff.

Then we had a neat thing happen—an unusual encounter—but I will let Leah share that with you in another chapter.

All in all, the Lord's hand was involved in everything we did. This included His promise, His plan, and yes, even His process and His provision.

These are just some of the things that we learned in walking in Steps of Faith! May each of you be blessed as you begin *your* walk!

A Close Encounter
of the "Unusual" Kind

Leah

EN-COUNT-ER, n. Latin meaning from the King James Dictionary: Contra, against, or rather recontre. Defined as a meeting particularly a sudden or accidental meeting of two or more persons.

At last, the writing of the book was completed! The book was written, and then edited by our friend, Suzanne Graham.

Thank you, Suzanne Graham!

We then began to search for the "right" publisher. First of all, we realized that we needed to learn as much as we could about the publishing industry. Where would we look to find a company that was "perfect" for us? The most important to us was that the publishing company we chose should be a Christian company. Also important, we wanted an ethical company with a good reputation. After looking at many companies, we settled on Tate Publishing in Oklahoma to bring our book to reality.

After the book was published, Brian and I were thrilled to also be given the privilege of recording an audiobook for *From Misery to Ministry—A Walk of Faith*. We were invited to travel to Mustang, Oklahoma, home of Tate Publishing, to do so. It was a great trip, and we accomplished a lot.

With the audio book available as an alternative to purchasing a physical book, people would be able to *hear* our story directly from Brian and me! I believed that it would be more personal to have each chapter read by the one who wrote it—a sort of validation—hearing the story in our own words.

The day came, and Brian and I were there, at Tate Publishing. When we parked our truck, there was a personalized sign on the front door of the building that said: Tate Publishing Welcomes Authors Brian and Leah Foutz.

We certainly felt special! Shauna was our "handler" for the recording. She met us at the door, ushered us inside the building, showed us where we were to go, and explained the instructions for making the recording. The first day we wanted to meet a few of the creative people who had worked on our book's preparation for publishing, so Shauna graciously spent some time introducing us to key people who made the book become a reality. It was wonderful to put faces with the voices we had heard on the phone. We were glad that we had some time to visit with them.

Shauna then took us into the main room, which was designated for the graphic artists and audio-visual technicians. In the corner of this room were two small sound booths used for recording the audio tapes and discs for books written by Tate authors.

The booths were small, just large enough for one person to go in and sit down. There was a microphone, headphones, and a computer. The setup was ready to go, and so were we! Sound engineers would put it all together later.

When day one of recording came to a close, we were more than half finished. We were pretty tired, especially with the travel of the previous two days, but pleased with how well it had gone. Recording the audiobook was tedious in some ways, but in other ways it was really fun. Brian and I were told to return the next morning to finish reading the final chapters.

A neat thing happened on day two. We had prayed early that morning that our recording time would be productive and that we would finish by the early afternoon. Brian started first in the booth again, recording the audio on one of his chapters, and then it was my turn. We were having so much fun that before we knew it, we were done! We had actually finished reading and recording all of the chapters. Wow! That seemed quick! Now it would be up to the audio staff to work their magic and put it all together.

Our final destination at Tate was a meeting with Jim Miller, our marketing representative. We went over to the main office, which was across the street, to meet with him. We arrived in the main foyer and the secretary called Jim to come to the front.

He arrived shortly, and took us into a conference room so that we could visit with him for a few minutes. It didn't take much time for us to feel very comfortable and relaxed. We chatted with one another easily, enjoying our time together.

All at once, the conference room door opened, and a man walked in. We could not see his face due to the fact that his arms were filled to overflowing with books of all sizes! As he entered the room, he spoke to us from somewhere behind the pile of books saying, "Don't mind me, I'll be gone in a minute!"

We watched in amusement as he slowly inched toward a closet at the rear of the room. When he got to the door of the closet, he opened it and began to put the books inside. All of a sudden, books began slipping from his grip and cascading out of the closet! As he bent over to pick them up, he said again, "I'm okay…I'll be out of here in a minute."

The scene reminded me of the part in the movie *The Wizard of Oz*, where Dorothy and her menagerie arrive in the Emerald City to meet with the Great Oz. As they slowly approached The Oz, Toto the dog ran over to a curtain and pulled it aside to reveal a man working the controls of the machinery used to create the fearful image of the Wizard. His comment to Dorothy and the others was to "Pay no attention to the man behind the curtain!"

Of course, for us, the minute he told us not to pay attention to him, we were all riveted, watching him gather and restack the books within the closet! Jim chuckled and commented, "Well, Brian and Leah, meet Dr. Tate! This man is the founder of Tate Publishing Company!"

Dr. Tate emerged from the closet minus the books. Introductions were made, and chuckles enjoyed as we discussed his entrance. We then spent some time talking with him, learning how he had started the company.

I recalled our looking for and researching publishing companies. This research included the dos and don'ts of publishing, as well as the differences between traditional and self-publishing. One of the most important concerns for us was choosing a trustworthy company that would honor Christ. We also wanted a company we could trust with the story of Victoria's life. After much research and prayer, we felt that Tate Publishing was the best choice for us.

As Dr. Tate began to share with us about starting the company, he told us how he and his company reviewed any and all comments from their authors (positive or negative), both through author testimonials and comments made on the internet.

This was really neat to know because we had seen some negative comments about the company posted online and had some questions in this area. Now here we were, getting answers to those questions before they were even asked. After hearing all of this information we felt that we had chosen the right publishing company for us. Yes, we had a wonderful time at Tate Publishing!

Both of us felt that our visit with Dr. Tate was great. As Brian would later say, "This was a divine encounter." We told Dr. Tate that he and all the people we worked with had made us feel quite comfortable during our visit.

It was quite amusing to have met the founder of the company in such a manner. After visiting with us for several minutes, it was time for him to leave, and for us to complete our meeting with Jim. Dr. Tate did not seem to be rushed at all—in fact, he personally awarded us two Tate coffee cups to remember him by!

Of course, Brian and I *will* remember Dr. Tate, but for his poise, his quick wit, and his sense of humor—*not* the falling books or the coffee cups! It was a fitting end to our wonderful two days at Tate Publishing.

> Consider it all joy, my brethren, when you encounter various trials, knowing that the testing of your faith produces endurance. And let endurance have its perfect result, so that you may be perfect and complete, lacking in nothing. (James 1:2–4, NASB)

Trusting in the Lord

Leah

> Trust in the Lord with all your heart and lean not on
> your own understanding; in all your ways submit to
> him, and he will make your paths straight.
>
> —Proverbs 3:5–6 (NASB)

Have you ever had a day when you really don't want to do anything at all? Well, today is one of those days for me—a slow, lazy day. On top of that, the internet connection isn't working on my computer right now, and I am feeling quite "disconnected" (pun *intended*. Ha!). It seems like there's always something that we *need* to do or *should* do. Actually, I think we are usually more limited by what we *can* and *cannot* do.

What a shame. Has our creativity begun to wane? Once upon a time, when we were kids, we would figure out something to do, or say, or write, or play-act. Then we would be busy doing that for hours and hours. Nowadays, if we aren't working at our jobs or at home doing something else, we tend to sit in front of a computer screen or television and let *it* entertain us! What a waste of precious time that is! Seems that we don't even have an original thought at times. We think we must surf the internet to find something to do.

Why do we do that? Is it because there truly *isn't* anything else to do, or have we begun to assume that someone or some*thing* (like a computer or a television) is responsible for telling us what to do, what to say, and how to act? How sad is that?

People who lived during Biblical times had no computers. Heck, they didn't even have electricity! And yet, they were able to keep themselves busy and/or entertained. After all the chores were done, did they play sheep-tossing games, or rock-tossing games to see who could hurl a rock the farthest?

Even though they had to be diligent to till their land and plant the seeds for God to grow, and then reap the crops when they were ripe, I believe that they also made time for relaxing. There was time set aside for praying, singing, and playing. However, those things were always *after* their basic needs were met, not before.

They truly had to depend on God for even the most necessary things, even their food. We are so spoiled these days. We are used to hopping into a car, driving to a food store, and *buying* food that has already been grown by someone else. What spoiled people we are!

Farming was hard work. At least 90 percent of people in the ancient world lived by working the land. When planting time came, the people would pray for God's help with growing their crops. God was always a huge factor in farming. If He did not cause rain to fall, the seeds would not grow, and there would not be food to eat.

"To sow" means to scatter seed over the ground. Here are some notes concerning farming that I read in a book called *Bible Archeology* concerning farming back then:

> Sowing took place after the first rains had softened the ground. If the farmer tried to plough before the rain, the plough-blade could not dig into the ground. First, the farmer would have to plough the ground, then he carried a basket or pouch attached to the waist and threw the seeds across the dirt. The idea was that GOD would see the seeds and cause them to grow! How's that for different?
>
> In that time there were two methods of sowing seed: by broadcasting (throwing out) the seeds by hand, or a seed-drill. For the first method, the farmer walked along the furrows at a constant pace pulling handfuls of seed from a bag at his side and throwing them over the soil.
>
> Later, when the seeds began to take root, the farmer would return and plow up the rows again, so that the sprouted seedlings could be buried under the soil and grow. Sometimes the farmer would do this by dragging branches or a log behind a team of oxen.
>
> Several people might be involved for the second method: one to direct the plough and push the handle down into the soil, one to direct the animals, and a third person to hold the seed bag on his shoulder and drop the seeds into the funnel which pointed down

> to the soil. These seeds would fall behind the plough-point, so that they were covered by the falling soil.
>
> That I will give the rain of your land in its season, the former rain and the latter rain, that you may gather in your grain, and your new wine, and your oil…
>
> Take heed to yourselves, lest your heart be deceived, and you turn aside, and serve other gods, and worship them; and the anger of Yahweh be kindled against you, and he shut up the sky, so that there shall be no rain. (Deut. 11:14; 16–17a, WEB)

One of the things that I have learned since we moved out into the countryside is that there truly are people whose *occupation* is farming! These farmers spend hours upon hours planting, tilling, watering, and watching their crops. They are ready to kill bugs, worms, and any other pests that might show up and destroy their crops. They are even pretty "watchful" of neighbors as well.

As I watched how our closest neighbor tended his crops, knowing that his wife would be "putting up" (or storing) the bounty to be eaten at a later date, I marveled at how much farmers must trust our Lord. If they don't get enough rain, they have to use their own precious water supplies to keep the plants growing. If they get too much rain, the crops can be ruined, which means less food to eat during the winter months.

I believe that even the huge commercial enterprises that grow food for so many people to purchase at grocery stores must rely upon God's grace to help them have success in their efforts. Isn't that interesting? We can look back and see how hard it was for people long ago to grow crops to live. However, today we must still trust God to provide the rain to water the crops and the sun to help them to grow, unless they are being grown inside a climate-controlled garden. Yet, even though these plants are grown in the perfect environment, it *still* takes *God's* hand to make the plants grow!

I believe that God wants us to look to Him for our sustenance for *everything!* God made us in His image, and expects us to look to Him for everything we may need.

There was a time when Brian and I had no choice but to rely completely upon the Lord. We had some unexpected expenses come up, and used up almost *all* our cash as well as most of our savings. I mean nearly *every* penny that was in that account! As a friend might have said, "We ain't just a-wolfin'!"

Like many of us, our last resort was to *pray*. After exhausting our own ideas, we asked our Lord for the provisions. Brian was still working and had several life insurance cases pending, but he had not been paid yet (oh, the joy of working in an all-commission business).

It seemed that there was more out-go than income. We found ourselves praying deeply, asking the Lord to hear our pleas and help us.

Learning to trust Him is very hard because we are human. But we have found that the Lord wants the best for us, and if we just ask Him, trust Him and *believe* that He will provide. That belief comes from His Word and really hits the mark:

> Therefore I tell you, whatever you ask for in prayer, believe that you have received it, and it will be yours. (Mark 11:24, NIV)

On the drive to church that day we talked about where we were financially, spiritually, and physically, and how Brian had been feeling. It had been very hard for him, dealing with constant back pain.

Again, I reminded him that the Lord had already healed him by His stripes, and that he was just waiting on the manifestation of that healing. Brian was still leading with his soul, or his head—it's our nature—but we had been learning more and more each day to give up that first moment of time to Him, to be led by Him, and to be used by Him.

On this particular weekend when we got to church, we had a "God-moment"—another step of faith in which our Lord revealed Himself to us:

During our welcome-time, I went off to meet and greet other church members and visitors. When I returned to my seat, there was an envelope with a card in it. I looked around to see if anyone was watching me, but it was just me.

I sat down and I opened up the envelope and pulled out a card. The front of the card said, "PEACE—Peace I leave with you—My peace I Give you—JESUS."

Inside of the card it read:

"Praying the Lord will comfort you with His peace,
Surround you in His love,
And encourage you with His Presence."

Then, in hand-printed letters was the following: "The Lord said to give this to you...Love in Christ."

A piece of folded paper was inside. When I opened it I found a cashiers' check for $1,000. WOW! The Lord gave us $1,000! *Wow!*

I just sat there and wept. I was too stunned to move, so I just sat there in awe with nothing to say.

When Brian returned to our seats, I asked him if he knew who placed this envelope on our pew. He said, "What envelope?" I then showed him the card. He opened the envelope and read the card. Then he opened the folded piece of paper and began to weep. As far as we knew, other than a few prayer requests, we had not shared how terrible things were for us, but *God* knew!

We looked at several people sitting near us and began asking if they had seen who had put a card on our pew, but nobody had seen anything! There was no name from who gave us the card, only a cashiers' check with our names on it.

Later, when we got home, Brian recalled an email I had gotten, in which our friend Anthony Hall shared part of a Word with me.

Anthony had said he could see God providing for us and our ministry, *in abundance*. He went on, saying this: "Share with Brian that we (both Brian and me) are to *listen* to God and He will direct our paths; we are not to be as Abram was: he heard God tell him to go to a new land, but when Abram got there, he did not stay. He went further on, and then God had to bring him back to the right place. This passage is found in Genesis 12–13." He closed out his email with, "Leah, speak the following over the two of you: Prosper and be in health—even as your soul prospers."

We were absolutely astonished! Of course, I started to weep, so touched by this *obvious* answer to our prayers!

As you can expect, Brian and I were *very* thankful for this very quick and obvious sign that the Lord had heard our prayers. We were able to pay the rent. Shortly after that Sunday, enough funds came in to get us back on our feet quickly. All I could say was, "What a wonderful God we serve!" As I like to tell others, "God is never late, He is always on time!"

> "And God is able to provide you with every blessing in abundance, so that you may always have enough of everything and may provide in abundance for every good work." (2 Cor. 9:8, RSV)

God *wants* to be part of our lives! When we, as His creation, His children, ignore Him and all He has done for us, I believe it grieves Him. According to the Bible, He made us (humans) to be higher than all the other animals here on earth, and He waits for us to acknowledge that fact.

Without His help, we would have *nothing*! It is true that, without God's help, none of us would be here. We should always be praising and thanking Him for His help, as well as acknowledging our connection with Him.

> So then it does not depend on the man who wills or the man who runs, but on God who has mercy. (Rom, 9:16, NASB)

Our dependence upon God does not demean us—it strengthens us! When we get that Truth into our minds and cherish it in our hearts, God is pleased with our growth toward maturity in Him. Through reading His Word and following the example of Jesus Christ, His Son, we can begin to be more like the people that God created us to be.

We can "walk in the garden" with Him daily, and manifest all of His wonderful, loving characteristics because we *know* Him. What a wonderful goal! To know Him that well, that closely. We become more like Him daily—truly a worthy goal! Look to be more like our God, and you *will* be blessed.

I pray that each of us will begin to *look* for God's presence in our daily lives, from the biggest things to those things that seem to be so insignificant. I have learned that God *wants* to be an active part of our lives every day! He is interested in our thoughts, our dreams, and everything else that pertains to our lives. He cares for us in a way similar to how a farmer cares for his crops: pruning us, plucking out the "weeds" in our lives, fertilizing us with His Truth, and watering us with His Love.

God wants us to know Him intimately, to be open with Him in every single moment that we are alive here on this earth. It gives God such pleasure to help us to learn to live more and more like Jesus, God's Son who came to earth to show us how to live for God the Father. The only thing we have to do is trust in Him and do our best to live our lives here on earth in a way that is pleasing to God the Father. When we are doing that, God is pleased with us, and blesses the things that our minds, hearts, and hands do. Look to Him today, and ask what *you* can do for Him!

God's Plan for Us

Brian

> O Lord, You are my God; I will exalt You, I will give
> thanks to Your name; For You have worked wonders,
> Plans formed long ago, with perfect faithfulness.
>
> —Isaiah 25:1 (NASB)

Isn't it amazing how most of us go through life, deciding what *we* will do and what *we* will become? We begin getting ideas in early childhood about what we want to be when we get older.

Children may say they want to become a police officer, a fireman, a doctor, a banker, a builder, or an artist. In time, some will go on to make a reality of those childhood dreams. Yet others will do something totally different, looking for work that will bring them money, power, and fame.

Sadly, there will be those who give up and do not know what they want. Like tumbleweeds of the deserts and plains, they will go to and fro with no desire or passion.

In Proverbs 16 there is a powerful statement that reveals God's plan for our lives:

> A man's mind plans his way, but the Lord directs his
> steps and makes them sure. (Prov. 16:9, AMP)

God does have a plan for each of us! As Dr. Myles Munroe said, "We need to ask God for the vision that He has for our lives.

"What you were designed to be known for is your gift. God has put a gift or talent in every person that the world will make room for. It is this gift that will enable you to fulfill your vision. It will make a way for you in life. It is in exercising this gift that you will find real fulfillment, purpose, and contentment in your work. It is interesting to note that the Bible does not say that a man's education makes room for him, but that his gift does."

I am reminded of God's promise for us:

> For I know the plans that I have for you, declares the
> Lord, plans for welfare and not for calamity to give
> you a future and a hope. (Jer. 29:11, NASB)

As a child, I was taught the basics of music. This I would recognize later as a gift from God. This gift would take me through junior and senior high school and for a brief time through college.

This special gift of music would be something that the Lord would give back to me years later as an adult.

I can remember looking back at an autobiography that I had to write when I was in sixth grade. While reading this fun and interesting piece of history, I came across something that really stunned and amazed me. I have no idea where the thought came from, or why, of all things, I wrote this.

The paper said that I wanted to grow up and become an oilman. It also said that I wanted to own an oil company. It said I wanted to do this because I wanted help others and make a difference in the world. Wow! And this all came from the mind and heart of a twelve year old.

Growing up, I would graduate from high school and begin college. I thought I really wanted to be a professional musician. My mother said, "Well, that is a pretty tough thing to do, and you probably won't make much money. So you need a back up plan. Get a music teaching degree so that if things don't work out you can always teach." Wow—thanks, Mom. Then she would finish off her thought with, "Become the best you can be."

I dropped out of college at the beginning of my junior year. Why, you might ask? Well, I had no money, and I had no vision. No heart, no passion, and no desire. Later I would move back home to live with my mother and her husband in Texas. For a year I did heavy construction work, learning all sorts of new things. Things that I did not care for and that I was not made to do.

I then found a job in the retail automotive parts and supply business. I had no love or desire to work on cars, but I found that God had given me a great memory.

I was able to learn and recognize the different type of parts and to look those parts up in a catalog. For some unknown reason, the auto parts catalogs and I became great friends. I enjoyed helping customers find the right parts for their cars and trucks. Over the years, I would teach and train other men and women in working the auto parts supply business.

> The Lord is near to the brokenhearted and saves the crushed in spirit. Many are the afflictions of the righteous, but the Lord delivers him out of them all. (Ps. 34:18–19, ESV)

As time passed, I began seeing that I really needed help. No, not with the auto supply business, but with me, personally. I could handle success with money and casual relationships with people, but I was not good with people in my personal life and especially in my love life. It seemed that personal relationships were one disaster after another.

Finally on July 15, 1981, after a few more failed relationships and fears of my future and as well as other worries, I attended a concert at Del Mar Stadium in Houston, Texas.

I went to hear Sandi Patti and The Imperials perform. It was super! It was awesome! At one point, the music stopped playing and I figured that the bands were going to take a break.

Suddenly, this guy walks out on the stage. He introduced himself as Pastor John Bisagno of First Baptist Houston. He walked up to the microphone and began speaking. "Boy, wasn't that great! Please stay seated, I have a short message to share with you and then the band will be back to play some more."

Okay, I can do this! I said to myself. *I can listen to a short message and then the band will be back!*

Pastor John did give a message, and it did not seem very long.

He said things about life, doing the right thing, and being the best, and that we all far short because of sin. As he spoke, it was as if he was looking into my life, all the things that I had done wrong, and all my fears and doubts about life. When he finished speaking, he told people that if they wanted to start over in life, to come down front and ask Jesus into their heart.

I just sat there. I was waiting for the band to come back. Then suddenly, I had this strange feeling come over me. Out of nowhere, it was as if there was someone standing in front of me. I could not see them but I felt like someone was there. Then…I felt something.

I did not know what to do. It felt like someone stuck a hand into my stomach and reached to the back of my inside and gently pulled me up out of my seat. I was suddenly standing. And then I felt this same hand began pulling me gently to the aisle.

The next thing that I knew, I was walking down the platform stairs, then down to the main ground on the football field. And there standing around many other people, a short man came up to me. He gently spoke to me and helped me say the sinner's prayer, and I gave my life to Jesus Christ. There, on that open field, my life would be changed forever.

I like the way that the Apostle Paul shares with us about coming to Jesus Christ:

> For with the heart one believes and is justified, and with the mouth one confesses and is saved. (Romans 10:10, esv)

But then I looked up this same passage in the Message Bible. It *rocks*!

> With your whole being you embrace God setting things right, and then you say it, right out loud: God has set everything right between him and me! (Rom. 10:10, msg)

There is no higher high in life than when you give your life to Jesus Christ.

It is the main "game changer" in life. Nothing else even comes close.

Later, I would meet and marry my bride, Leah, and begin a new journey with her. In time, the earthly need for making money, being successful in business, living in nice places, and traveling became important things for me to strive for.

In March 1986, our only child Victoria Carol Foutz was born to us. A bundle of joy and fun.

In 1987, we began a series of hardships. Over the next couple of years, there would be a loss of finances, a bankruptcy, losing our home, and then the feeling of trauma. The feeling that I was now a failure.

The Lord would provide me with an attorney to walk us through this wilderness journey. I remember when I walked into his office, feeling rejected, and feeling like a pauper.

During our visit, he shared that God can change our position and place in life, and through Him we would find hope. He can take us through that period of restoration and prepare us for the next journey.

He would share with me the story of another man who struggled with little or no finances. The man lived in a small cabin out in the country, working to buy candles so that he could read books in the evening after coming home from work. He was doing the best he could. He would have failed relationships, failed businesses, and his sweetheart would die. He would be defeated in an election to Congress, then go on later to be elected. He would again be defeated in the Senate and defeated as a vice presidential candidate. But later, he would win the election as President of the United States of America. That man was Abraham Lincoln.

After hearing this story, I walked out of his office with my head held high, knowing that all things are possible with God. This would be a huge step of faith in my life.

In 1991 I began seeking the Lord more and more. The more I read and the more that I dug into His Word, the more He began changing things in my life. Our finances began improving. So did my outlook on life. I was learning to serve others, not to just sell them something or take care of an immediate need, but to really serve my fellow man.

The year 2004 would bring a season of trauma and grief as we lost our only daughter Victoria. But the Lord answered our prayers and brought us that supernatural peace that goes beyond all understanding.

Over the next few years, Leah and I started learning to be led more by the Holy Spirit. This was an act of faith and a process of learning more and more about who He is and why we are here.

This would become a step of faith, a prompting and leading of the Holy Spirit that would eventually move us from Katy to the beautiful rolling landscape and hillsides of New Ulm, Texas.

During one of our study lessons in February 2011, Leah and I were working through an amazing study by Chuck Pierce called *The 50 Days to Staking Your Claim*. Yes, it was literally a daily Bible study for fifty days. It was an incredible study and a life changer for both of us.

On this particular day we were reading in the book of Joshua 3–5. Chapter 3 really set the stage for us in our walk. As we studied, we both had the same Bible, a MacArthur Study Bible in the New American Standard Version.

Here we learned of Joshua crossing of the Jordan River, and like Moses, the Lord would pave the way—no pun intended!

You see, that current generation of Israel had not seen any miracles that God had done. Why? Because their parents and grandparents were disobedient to the Lord, and He had them all die in the wilderness.

But suddenly, as we were reading, something jumped out at me. I looked at Leah and said, "Wow! I just saw something here!"

"What's that?" she asked.

I then began pointing some things out to her in the scriptures. I was really excited and I felt a leaping my spirit.

I pointed out to her that in these chapters, the Lord showed three very important things to the people:

1. His Promise
2. His Plan
3. His Process

I shared with her that in looking back in our other studies of Abraham, Isaac, Joseph and Joshua that this same theme happens over and over.

> O Lord, You are my God; I will exalt You, I will give thanks to Your name; For You have worked wonders, Plans formed long ago, with perfect faithfulness. (Is. 25:1, NASB)

As we continued talking, I said, "We have to realize that in our daily walk, this same theme will play out over and over. All that we have to do is to be open, willing, and obedient!"

As Leah and I finished our study, we spent time in prayer. Praying is important in all things that you do. We prayed for our families, for our needs, and for His direction. After we finished our prayer, we began just talking with one another.

We were feeling that God was about to do some really amazing things in our lives. I did feel stressed out about our finances, but, as I shared with Leah, "I am not afraid, because I know that the Lord is taking care of us—and He will provide for us in every way!" Now here was something really strange. We could feel the earth move beneath our feet and we felt that something wonderful was about to happen.

I then told Leah, "I have never felt this way before and this is an amazing preparation for things yet to come." Then these words came out of my mouth, "His vision… His provision…His protection…His Projection…His position.

"You see, Leah, there is a plan for us. A time to write music, a time for prayer, a time to preach, a time to write, and a time to share God's love."

On this day and at this time, we began walking and talking in a new and different way, one totally different than before, realizing that each new day brings a new adventure and a new divine intersection.

There would be an intersection of hope, healing, and encouragement to help others.

And as we talked, I shared, "There is only today to be open, willing and obedient to be used by Him and for Him. This will require a step of faith for both you and me."

> I will instruct you and teach you in the way you should go; I will counsel you with my loving eye on you. (Ps 32:8, NIV)

Who's that knocking at my Door?

Leah and Brian

> Here I am! I stand at the door and knock. If anyone
> hears my voice and opens the door, I will come in
> and eat with that person, and they with me.
>
> —Revelation 3:20 (NIV)

Now, here's a thought from Leah: "There will be certain times and certain areas in your life when God will show up and let you know that He is there. Sometimes, He is knocking at our door, at other times *we* are doing the knocking. These are the times when the Lord will speak to you and let you know that He is there, right there in the midst of your life."

In 2008 I met Rev. France Brown at CBS (College of Biblical Studies) just after I had finished taking my pre-entry tests. He and I had a great conversation and enjoyed our informal meeting.

I shared with him that he had been to Grace United Methodist Church in Katy, Texas in 2005, and I had heard him preach a sermon on "Returning to Ziklag."

I missed hearing him in person because I had a prior commitment to play at Holy Cross Episcopal Church in Sugarland that Sunday, but I did get one of his tapes. I told him that I listened to the tape several times and shared it with other people as well.

France then said that there was a woman who came up to him after that service and shared that she had gone through her own Ziklag recently. He told me that this woman had just lost her only child and that his sermon ministered to her. He then said that the story had deeply touched him, and he did not understand how any woman would have gone through this and still be able to be up, moving around with a great spirit of healing.

As he finished telling me this story, I looked at him and said, "That would be my wife, Leah." He was taken aback and gave me his deepest sympathy.

The Lord then gave me an opportunity to share the rest of the story with him.

When we finished talking, he told me that he wanted to get back in touch with me; that we should have lunch and carry on our conversation at a later date.

We all need to learn to be open, willing, and obedient to listen to the Lord. There are so many treasures to be found when we are simply open for the Holy Spirit to work in us.

In late February 2009, I had an amazing phone call from my good friend Linda Moore. I had been sharing with her about a tugging in my heart. I felt a stirring in my spirit to have more of Him in my life; to become more open, willing, and obedient to be used by the Lord. I wanted to learn more about being led by the Holy Spirit and to help others, especially in the area of bringing hope, healing, and encouragement.

I shared with her about taking seminary classes and a desire to become an ordained minister. I felt that this was a calling on my life.

Linda then revealed something that I had never known about her. She said both she and her husband had been ordained as ministers through the Charles and Frances Hunter Ministries in Houston, Texas.

In fact, while she was talking to me she went on the internet and saw that the Hunter Ministries were holding a healing conference in three weeks in Porter, Texas. She suggested that this would be a great way for us to get more information on healing, and if we wanted to, we could be ordained as ministers through their organization. Wow! Way cool!

Leah and I talked about this next step: about learning more about healing and an opportunity to be ordained as ministers. We decided to lift this up in prayer and see where the Lord would lead us.

While we were on one of our drives the next day we discussed this event more. We both felt led to sign up and make the trip. Besides, Leah shared with me that she had always wanted to have a prayer language and the ability to speak to the Father in tongues.

After we returned from our drive I got on the phone, called the Hunter Ministries, and got us enrolled for their next class. This class would be held on March 12, 13, and end on the 14th.

The following Sunday, Leah and I visited some dear friends, Maisie and Bob, in a town nearby. We spent a lovely morning and afternoon with the two of them, as well as another couple that they knew. It was a great time of fellowship and just praising the Lord.

After lunch, the women stayed at the dining table while the men went out onto the screened-in porch to visit.

Little did the men know that the women were having a "God Experience"!

While the women were talking about being close to the Lord, the conversation turned to the gifts of the Spirit, and the fact that these gifts were available to all who asked for them, including the gift of other tongues.

Leah was especially interested in this gift, as she had prayed for a long time that the Lord would bless her with it someday. Little did she know that *today* was the day! The other ladies immediately asked her if she really wanted to receive the gift of other tongues, and Leah said, "Yes!"

They stood next to Leah, placed their hands on her, and began to pray in tongues for her. Leah agreed with them both, and in a very short time, she began to "test" the Spirit by opening her mouth and letting *Him* speak *through* her, if that's what He wanted her to do. Maisie told Leah that there was some very strong resistance while they were praying for this, and she felt that there was an evil spirit in the room that did *not* want Leah to receive this particular gift.

Immediately, all three women began to pray against that spirit, asking that the Lord take over and remove it. As Leah prayed with the others, she began to quietly open her mouth and just let the Spirit take over her words.

All of a sudden, Maisie began to smile as she listened to the wonderful sound of the Spirit speaking out of Leah's mouth. Wow! What a blessing! Maisie and her friend then asked Leah to continue to let the words flow out of her mouth. It was truly a special time of praise and thankfulness to the Lord.

> Therefore I say to you, all things for which you pray and ask, believe that you have received them, and they will be granted you. (Mark 11:24, NASB)

Later, as Leah and I were leaving, Maisie said to Leah, "Be sure to tell Brian about what happened to you today!"

I immediately asked what had happened, and when I found out what it was, I stopped the truck and called out to Maisie and her husband Bob. "That's not fair!"

Laughing, Maisie told me that if I wanted to receive the gift of tongues, Leah and I would have to come back soon. So off we went. What an amazing afternoon!

The following week Leah and I were back at Christian Faith Church, and who should show up? None other than Maisie and Bob! After church, Maisie and Bob invited us to go home and have lunch with them.

After a time of food and fellowship, Maisie looked at me and asked if I was ready to receive the gift of speaking in unknown tongues. I told her that I had been praying all week to have God give me this gift and felt that I was ready to receive it. That is, if He wanted me to have this gift.

I also shared that I had a yearning to become *more*—to be used more by God by becoming a minister and fulfilling His calling. Maisie, Leah, and Bob began to pray for the Lord to give me this gift.

With that, off we went into the living room where Bob, Maisie, and Leah sat me down and began praying with me. As we began, I was asking the Lord to fill me with His Spirit. As I was praying, I felt a strange pressure about me, almost like a dark resistance of some kind. The more that I prayed, I found myself weeping and crying out to God for His help. It felt like I was there for a half an hour and felt weak and lightheaded. Then, an amazing thing happened. My weeping was gone, and I was filled with joy and excitement. I began hearing something new, an utterance in my voice. My prayers had been answered!

Then I remembered what the Lord had said:

> John baptized with water, but you will be baptized with the Holy Spirit. (Acts 11:16, GNT)

March 12th came quickly and Leah and I headed out to Porter, Texas. It would be a long drive from Katy to Porter and back each day for the conference, but it was well worth it! We met so many amazing people who were from all over the world. There were some from New Zealand, Canada, and the USA.

Not only did we meet and learn about new friends, but the teaching was incredible!

When Saturday night came, something unique happened to us. While we were waiting for the program to begin, I looked underneath my seat and found a package with our names on it. I opened the package and found information on the Hunter Ministries, our nametags, and ordination license, but something else as well. There was a certificate that was being awarded to both Leah and me showing that on this day we were ordained as ministers.

But that was not the coolest thing. The coolest thing was that on the certificate was the date. Yeah, Brian, those certificates all have dates on them. Yeah, but it was the date that was so cool. You see, the date printed on our certificate is March 14, 2009. March 14th is our daughter's birthday.

What an amazing and wonderful reminder of God's love! This would be another adventure in steps of faith that were waiting for us.

> It was he who gave gifts to people; he appointed some to be apostles, others to be prophets, others to be evangelists, others to be pastors and teachers. He did this to prepare all God's people for the work of Christian service, in order to build up the body of Christ. (Eph. 4:11–12, GNT)

Autumn's Story: A New Season

Brian

> And He made from one man every nation of
> mankind to live on all the face of earth, having
> determined their appointed times and the boundaries
> of their habitation, that they would seek God, if
> perhaps they might grope for Him, though He is not
> far from each one of us, for in Him we live and move
> and exist, as even some of your own poets have said,
> "For we are also His children."
>
> —Acts 17:26–28 (NASB)

We are constantly amazed by how the Lord will "set things up" behind the scenes. In taking steps in our faith walk, we have been blessed to witness how God's hand is in everything that we do.

During these past ten years, Leah and I have been through many seasons together. Not just the standard four seasons winter, spring, summer, and fall, but seasons with work, projects, friends, and ministry.

There was one season and an event that was so amazing that we did not see how God set things up until after the fact. When the Lord begins to move in your life, your business, and your family, remember to pray, listen for that small still voice, and be prepared in and out of season to be used by God.

Here is how God moved during one such ministry event in June 2012.

Our music ministry had been doing a special evening event at local churches called "An Audience of One." This was an evening where the ministry band played different kinds of music, sang songs, read scripture, had moments of open prayer, and played in the Spirit before our Lord and King.

He was our "Audience of One"!

There were no sermons, no collection plates, no special speaker, no announcements, and no agenda. We usually did not have an Invitation or a "come to Jesus" time at the altar. And, with the exception of Amazing Grace, we usually *did not play hymns*. Don't ask me why, we played hymns in church services but never at Audience of One. Remember this: it will pop up later in the story!

This was a time for people to come and sit and soak in His presence. They could come and go as they pleased, read their Bible, participate in singing, dance, lift their hands up to the Lord, come to the front and kneel and pray to God, or just stay in their seats.

The musicians would play worship songs, instrumental songs, individual guitar music, or keyboard music, contemporary Christian music creatively arranged for each Audience of One.

This particular event in June 2012 was being held at Christian Faith Church in Bellville, Texas. The pastor, Lynn Burling had approached me about six weeks before the event and said, "I know that you guys don't usually have a member of the local church play with you because you do not want it to be a sponsored church event. But I was just wondering…I would really love to sing with you guys. I don't want to speak or give a sermon, but I just feel led by the Spirit to ask you."

Being the leader of the ministry band, I am always open to anyone who is being led by the Spirit. I try to stay in tune (no pun intended) with whatever God is doing in people's lives. I spoke with Donna, our worship leader, and she said, "If he is being led by the Spirit to sing, I have no problem with that." So I called Lynn back and said, "No problem, dude…we would love to have you."

Lynn replied, "Just let me know when you are rehearsing and what you are singing, and I will be there. And Brian, thank you." Lynn would add an additional male vocal to the mix that blended extremely well for every song for the evening.

Little did we know that God had planned a special step of faith for everyone who would be attending, including the musicians!

With just over a month to go, I shared with Donna that the Lord had really been impressing upon me to do an arrangement of the hymn "Blessed Assurance" for the Audience of One.

In fact, several nights in a row He would wake me up and give me the arrangement. I finally went to the church and found a drum pad. (That is a special keyboard pad that has pre-programmed drum sounds—almost like you have a drummer in the house.) Since we did not have a drummer, we often used drum pads.

As it turned out that this particular keyboard drum pad would work just fine. We practiced with the new drum loop, and it really fit well with the song.

Donna would later share, "I looked at Brian, puzzled at the time, and said, 'Well, if that's what you feel God wants us to do, I guess we'll do it.'" So we proceeded to rehearse it and had our guitar player Stephen Coffee use his harmonica to "jazz it up."

After playing through the song, Donna shared that she was not sure about using the harmonica for the song. Stephen then shared that he had felt a strong prompting by the Holy Spirit to use the harmonica.

When Stephen said this, I sensed the same prompting and I could only say, "We have to use the harmonica!" Now here is where things really began to change—most of us did not know any of this until after The Audience of One had concluded.

With about two weeks to go, Donna was preparing scriptures (as was her normal routine) to compliment "the set" or list of songs that we were going to do for The Audience of One in Bellville on June 9, 2012.

One of the scriptures that God prompted her to include was John 3:16. Then, He had her write "Salvation Invitation" on her song sheet for "I Exalt Thee."

Donna said she really questioned this with God because Audience of One had never included this as part our events.

She would later share even more with us: "We promote it as a time to 'Sit and Soak' with no preaching or offering; just worship and scripture reading. But God kept urging me that *an invitation* was to be included in this Audience of One. So, I kept it in my notes."

At our final rehearsal before an Audience of One, Donna and I would meet for about 10–15 minutes and discuss the set of music, sometimes changing the order, adding a song, dropping a song, placing some extra instrumental music in different places, and always a scripture change. God does that.

During our pre-rehearsal meeting, Donna leaned over to me and said, "Brian, I know that we don't do this, but the Lord has really placed a heavy prompting on my heart. I believe that we are to have an Invitation to Salvation this time. I know that we don't do this, but for some reason, we are supposed to do this." Donna said that I looked very strangely at her, but said, "Uh…okay." I think that is all that I *could* say at that moment. I actually felt a jump in my spirit when she said this. So, we were going to give an Invitation for anyone who would like to receive Christ this time.

We continued getting ready for the event—practicing, working with Lynn, and getting the songs "tighter" as we musicians like to say. We wanted to play our best for the King, so we put a lot of time into getting ready.

The week before the event, Donna's sister Whitney received a phone call from her son, Luke who lived in Dayton, TX and was having some difficulties. Dayton is about an hour northeast of Bellville.

The locations are important here, so you will have to visualize a map.

Whitney lived in Brookshire, Texas. Donna lived in Katy, about an hour east of Bellville.

Apparently, Luke hadn't eaten in four days and called Whitney saying he was hungry and began to cry. He was broken and lonely, with nowhere to turn.

Whitney felt compassion for her son and said he just needed a break. She suggested that he should come visit her for a few days in Brookshire. As Whitney put it, this would allow Luke to "come into the Light." Luke did not have any transportation at the moment, so Whitney drove to Dayton to get him.

When Whitney got to Dayton, Luke asked his mother if his girlfriend Autumn could come along. Whitney agreed and they drove back to Brookshire.

Sometime later, Whitney called Donna and told her that Luke was there with her in Brookshire. Whitney told Donna that Luke really wanted to come and visit her (Donna) and her husband Wayne.

Donna would later share some really interesting things that were going on behind the scenes. Donna said, "So I invited Whitney and Luke over to dinner at our house in Katy. We decided that Wednesday evening would be a great time to meet."

Donna continued, "At this point, I had not been told anything about Autumn. When Whitney and Luke arrived, I was then introduced to Autumn. She was a young girl, and I was told that she was Luke's girlfriend. She seemed very quiet, said very little, but was polite during dinner. After dinner, we visited for a little while and they left."

Throughout the week, Whitney knew about our Audience of One and was talking to Luke and Autumn about it. Whitney explained this was just a time of music, singing, and Bible reading. There was no pressure, no message, no offering, and no hymns. Whitney really wanted them to hear Donna sing. Basically, no big deal.

Autumn then stunned Whitney with this statement: "I don't believe in God anymore, and I will not go to church ever again! You see four years ago, my best friend was shot and killed on the front doorsteps of our church."

Donna said, "As you can imagine, this must have been devastating to her, and she stopped believing in God." While at Whitney's, Autumn kept saying she was not going to go to the church. Whitney dropped the subject. Whitney was going, regardless.

Again, no one in the group knew anything about this behind-the-scenes activity.

Saturday, June 9th arrived. The ministry band was in Bellville getting prepared and we were all planning on an amazing evening with our special guest, our Lord and King!

Meanwhile, back in Brookshire, Whitney had a severe attack of vertigo. She's hadn't had an attack like this in a very long time. It was so bad she was unable to help Wayne's mother with her in-home care, and she was not able to drive her car.

This made Whitney extremely sad because she was really looking forward to Audience of One.

She told Luke and Autumn how disappointed she was that she couldn't go to the service.

Okay, this is where it becomes interesting. Autumn then said to Whitney, "Luke can drive your car. Why don't we take you? We'll wait outside the church and then drive you back home afterward." Whitney was totally surprised and delighted by this suggestion. So, that was the plan.

Boy! Now this was interesting! So off they went, with Luke and Autumn driving Whitney to Bellville.

Meanwhile, at the church in Bellville, we had all gathered together in the back room to begin praying for the evening and for one another.

Leah, my bride, who heads up our prayer ministry and is a prayer intercessor, called us all into prayer and began praying for the service. As was the usual practice, we would then pray for the person next to us on our left.

Benjamin Whitehead, who played with the church praise team came and ran sound for us. He gave a deep, heartfelt prayer of thanks to the Lord for giving me the vision for an Audience of One for the area, and for how it had become a reality. Also, that it would be successful in reaching out to many in the area. He prayed for the anointing God had placed, not only on my life, but on the others within the group—and for us being obedient to fulfill His vision. Wow! God, you are *awesome*!

> Yet a time is coming and has now come when the true worshipers will worship the Father in the Spirit and in truth, for they are the kind of worshipers the Father seeks. God is spirit, and his worshipers must worship in the Spirit and in truth. (John 4:23–24, NIV)

We closed out in prayer, praying for God's will to be done, and if there was anyone who was there tonight who did not know Him, that their heart would be opened and that they would invite Jesus Christ into their life.

We departed from the back room and headed out into the sanctuary, picked up our microphones and instruments, and prepared to start the evening with an Audience of One!

Later we would hear that when Whitney, Luke, and Autumn arrived, something began to change. Autumn was visibly shaking, and did not want to get out of the car. Apparently she was very fearful because of what had taken place in her past.

Whitney was thankful that God had provided her the transportation for The Audience of One. However, when she got out of the car, she immediately fell down in the parking lot. Her vertigo was nearly unbearable. Luke and Autumn had to help Whitney get inside the church building and then to a pew.

After they entered, Whitney shared that Luke and Autumn sat with her, but Autumn was visibly shaking. She was incredibly nervous and uncomfortable.

The time had finally arrived, and we began our service. Donna would open up the service with a prayer while I played an original instrumental keyboard song. Donna then finished the prayer and all the people said "Amen!"

Then, the ministry band began with the old hymn, "Blessed Assurance." Autumn was shocked! She looked at Whitney and said, "I thought you said that they don't do hymns!"

Whitney was also shocked. "They don't…I don't know what happened." What could she tell her? As far as she knew, we did not play hymns. She had been to Audience of One a couple of previous times. Oops!

Okay, now you are thinking, well maybe since it was just *one* song—she should be okay by now. But wait! there is more.

The very next song that we sang was another great hymn, "Wonderful Merciful Savior"!

Later I looked out and saw Autumn. She was now bent over with her hands on the pew in front of her, weeping deeply. She could not even look up. Most of the band did not see this because we are all engaged in playing and singing for Him. (I sometimes gaze out into the congregation to see how God is moving in people's lives—it is an awesome experience!)

By the third song, Autumn was really crying. Whitney later told us that she leaned over to Luke and said, "I have to leave, *now!*" With that, Autumn and Luke exited the building. Both Donna and I saw her leave.

We would later hear from Lynn that he also saw her leave, and more. Lynn said that the Lord had told him to be praying hard that a young lady would be saved tonight. He had looked out into the audience and knew everyone else who was there—*this* had to be the young lady. Lynn then shared, "At one point, the Spirit was so strong, I just bowed my head while singing, and I began praying in the Spirit for the girl."

Lynn said, "I knew that if God told me that this woman was to be saved—that this was the night—God's word never comes back void! I did not know where the girl was, but I just knew that I had to keep praying for her!"

Donna would share with us later, "I knew in my spirit that God was doing something here. I kept praying for guidance and proceeded with our program as planned." Wayne told me that he felt that Autumn was familiar with Christianity by her reaction to the music. He could tell she was feeling the draw as well and wanted to run away. We continued on with the program as planned. We were still playing for An Audience of One for our Most High King!

Donna would later tell us, "When we got to 'I Exalt Thee,' I gave the Salvation Invitation as I believed God wanted me to do. I knew that all of those sitting in the building at the moment, were 'believers,' but I continued to pray and sing anyway, just as we had it scripted it out."

Now during this time, I was playing my keyboard. I was looking out into the audience. As I looked around to see who was there, I begin to count each person. As I looked at each person, I suddenly found myself saying, "saved… saved…saved…saved" about each one. Everyone still left inside the church was saved, unless someone had been lying to themselves and to us all this time! The ones who were not saved had done an Elvis number. "They have left the building!"

I felt like there was an invitation, but no one was there to receive it. Pastor Lynn would tell me on the phone later in the week that he too felt like Donna was just preaching to the choir.

Now, back on the platform, we were still playing but we were getting close to the end of the Audience of One.

Donna said, "I saw Whitney get a phone call and leave the building. When she returned, Luke and Autumn were with her, and this time Autumn sat beside Whitney."

We had now come to the end of our set list and were ready to conclude the service. Then, out of nowhere, Pastor Lynn looked at Donna and said that he wanted to say something. Donna looked over at me and motioned that Lynn wanted to say something, and I nodded my head in affirmation to let him go ahead.

Lynn said, "I am feeling that I am being prompted by the Holy Spirit to continue with an Invitation of Salvation."

Keep in mind that Pastor Lynn was not here in the capacity of "pastor" this evening. He was only planning to be there to sing with us, but obviously God had other plans.

As Lynn began speaking, the Lord was moving mightily! My head bowed, I was looking down at the keyboard, and I was just flowing in the Spirit of what the Lord would have me play.

Still playing quietly in the background, at one point I heard Pastor Lynn say, "I remember that Brother Brian once shared that if you would like to come down for prayer, just cup your hands and someone will come and pray with you."

When I heard this, I said to myself, *Wow!* This was something that I learned from Pastor Jim Leggett at Grace UMC in Katy. I remembered sharing that same illustration three years ago, when I had preached my first sermon in this church before we came to join Christian Faith Church. Go, God!

As Pastor Lynn talked, Autumn leaned over to Whitney and asked, "Are they talking to me?" Whitney said to her that she was not sure, and Autumn needed to see what her heart was telling her. Pastor Lynn continued to talk, explaining something Brian had said at a previous Audience of One— about coming forward for prayer and "cupping your hands."

Autumn leaned over to Whitney again asking, "I think they are talking to me! What should I do?" Whitney encouraged her to follow her heart.

Autumn was afraid and asked Whitney to go with her to the front. When they got to the front, Autumn was still unsure of herself. Whitney motioned for her to cup her hands.

When I looked up, there was Autumn standing with Whitney. Autumn was looking at Whitney and making a motion with her hands. She seemed to show that she did not know if she was holding her hands right, or how to cup them. Whitney moved next to her and moved her hands into position and held them like drinking water—like a cup.

My bride Leah would later share that Autumn was there to get her cup *filled* from the Lord!

I turned to Leah and ask her to go down to pray with them as I did not feel it would be appropriate for me to leave from playing the keyboard. As Leah was making her way down, Pastor Lynn also went straight down to pray with them.

Donna said, "It is at this moment I begin praying in the Spirit and heard incredible singing in my head (and it's not coming from my voice). I'm praying in the Spirit for Autumn, and when I open my eyes, Autumn is glowing. I know that the singing I heard was the Angels in heaven, rejoicing in the return of a lost lamb. I begin free worship singing and Brian got my cue to return to 'I Exalt Thee.'"

> For I know the plans that I have for you declares the Lord, plans for welfare and not for calamity to give you a future and hope. Then you will call upon Me and come and pray to Me, and I will listen to you. You will seek Me and find Me when you search for Me with all your heart. (Jer .29:11–13, NASB)

Whitney would share with Donna later, "On the ride home, Autumn was 'floating' and excited about everything. I told her a little about Brian and Leah's story, about how they wrote a book about it. Autumn asked for a copy of the book to read, and I later blessed her with a copy."

I would get a long email from Donna later that week. Here is more of what she had to share.

"The important thing to keep in mind in this entire story is that I only met Autumn for the first time four days before and did *not* know anything about her. I found out all this information on Sunday afternoon after the fact." Whitney believes that God allowed the vertigo attack so that He could get Autumn to church. Remember, it was Autumn's idea to have Luke drive his mother to church.

"We need to keep them all in our prayers, and I'll do my best to encourage them at every turn. I'll also try to go help them find a church where they can continue to be spiritually fed and fellowship with other believers," Donna wrote.

All I can say is our God is an awesome God, and I'm so glad that we were obedient to our promptings from the Lord. The moral of the story is, "Never question God. He always has a plan. We just need to stay out of the way."

> It is He who changes the times and the epochs; He removes kings and establishes kings; He gives wisdom to wise men and knowledge to men of understanding. It is He who reveals the profound and hidden things; He knows what is in the darkness, and the light dwells in Him. (Dan 2:21–22, NASB)

When this season was over and we were able to go back and actually see how the pieces of the puzzle came together, Jeremiah's words rang loud and clear. When you seek Me, you will find me!

It took a girl named Autumn to show us how to abide in Him and trust Him, as we are led by the Spirit to take steps of faith through the seasons of life. Wow!

When you are able to go back and see how God works, you also will begin to realize that you—yes, you—are taking steps in your faith to be open, willing, and obedient to be used by Him!

God's Redirection

Brian

> Also with moisture He loads the thick cloud; He
> disperses the cloud of His lightning. It changes
> direction, turning around by His guidance, that it
> may do whatever He commands it on the face of the
> inhabited earth.
>
> —Job 37:11–12 (NASB)

If God is able to change the direction of the clouds, can He *not* do the same thing with man?

Did you ever have one of those days when you have planned out your day, all is going well…then suddenly, everything seems to take a new twist?

One Friday morning in May of 2011, my day started out just like that.

I am reminded of the line from the old TV series with Walter Cronkite called *You Are There*. The program would talk about true life stories that had happened in history. Cronkite would tell the viewers what was about to happen, then an announcer would give the date and the event, followed by a loud, "You are there."

All things were normal and then suddenly changed. A new direction was taken…and *you are there*!

Today would be like all other days—except you are there!

Someone once said that there will be distractions and obstacles in life, and those obstacles can be sometimes from the enemy and sometimes from God. I had to stop and think about this one for a minute, and decided to see what that word "distraction" really meant.

The word distraction means:

1. The act of distracting or the condition of being distracted.

2. Something, especially an amusement that distracts.

3. Extreme mental or emotional disturbance or obsession

But here is something to remember: God is not the author of confusion or a God of doubt. He is the creator, and by His hand, He can direct our steps.

> A person's steps are directed by the Lord. How then can anyone understand their own way? (Prov. 20:24, NIV)

If He can direct our path, then He can redirect our steps. Sometimes redirection of our steps will protect us from the enemy—take us around a potential harm or danger. He can also re-direct our steps, because He has something planned ahead for us, or something really cool to show us. He is awesome that way.

> In all thy ways acknowledge him, and he shall direct
> thy paths. (Prov. 3:6, KJV)

Now back to the divine direction that took place in my life on a beautiful day in May of 2011.

It was a Friday morning and I got up early, showered, and headed out from The Hill. My day would be somewhat full, especially in the morning.

You see, this morning I was going in to see my friend Alan Litvak for a breakfast meeting in Katy, Texas. This would be an early breakfast, so I needed to be there by 7:00 a.m. That meant I was up at 5:00 a.m. to be ready to leave by 5:45 a.m. Yes, it was an hour-and-fifteen-minute drive one way from here.

My destination was the Panera Bread restaurant in Katy, where I met Alan.

After some coffee and fellowship with Alan, David Vigil showed up and Alan left for an appointment.

David's daughter Lauren had been a close friend of our daughter Victoria. When those two girls got together, they were known as the Super-Duper-Hyper-Girls, and boy, were they ever! David actually led one of the young men to Christ at the altar during Victoria's service. That was an awesome day!

During my meeting with David, a number of other friends of ours showed up, and we all had a great visit. A couple of the men purchased a copy of our book while

I was there. Afterward, I went by our bank and made several deposits.

My last stop would be short and brief. (Ha-ha!) There was a young woman named Kristy who worked in a doctor's office not far from the bank. We had met her when Leah broke her ankle.

The young woman had lost her brother some time earlier in the year. Her father had been very ill: first a heart attack and then other medical challenges. She was living with her mother, and her life seemed to be in turmoil. She had wanted to buy a copy of our book from us, but finances made that impossible.

During this time, Ralph, one of our closest friends and who is like a son to us, had blessed us with a love offering in addition to purchasing some of our books.

He said in his letter, "Please use the extra money to bless a couple of other people with your book. Let the Lord direct you on whom to bless."

When I arrived at the office, I started toward the bathroom. But I changed my mind and went first to see Kristy and drop off the book.

I stood there at the front desk waiting – no one was there, but I could hear voices in the background. One of those was Kristy's.

Finally a young woman came up and asked how she could help me. I said, "My name is Brian Foutz, and I am here to see Kristy."

She said that Kristy had a family emergency and had to go home. Even though I had heard Kristy's voice in the back, and it seemed strange, I decided not to tell her that I had heard Kristy's voice.

I told the young woman that Kristy had shared with us that she had lost a brother, that my wife and I had written a book together since losing our only daughter, and that someone had bought a couple of extra books and wanted us to bless someone who could really use the book.

So we decided to bless Kristy with one. She then asked me what my name was, and for some dumb reason all I could say was, "My name is on the front cover." Duh!

So I left. Since I had to get gas for the Durango, I considered waiting and using the bathroom at the gas station. But for some unknown reason, I decided to follow my original plan. Just as I was getting ready to walk into the bathroom, I heard this voice in the hallway. "Mr. Foltz! Mr. Foltz!" Remembering that people have really botched up my name since childhood, I knew it could not be anyone else but me. "Yes, here I am," I yelled.

I turned and there was Kristy, standing in the middle of the hallway.

She just stood there, looking at me, somewhat in shock. As I began to approach her, she immediately ran into my arms, hugged me, and just cried and cried. Wow! I was thinking, *all this*…for just a book!

But she continued to keep crying. I held onto her and told her that it would be okay. Then she looked up into my eyes, crying, and said, "They just called me this morning and told me that my father was pronounced brain-dead." I just stood there for a second holding her, telling her that I was sorry.

Then I reached into my wallet, took out one of my cards, and asked, "Do you have a pen?"

She did not, so we walked back into the doctor's office. The first nurse that I had spoken to said, "I am so sorry, sir, I really thought she had left the building."

I said, "That's okay. I heard her voice, but I figured that she was not available."

Then, I got a pen from the desk and wrote down all of our phone numbers. "Here," I said. "Please feel free to call us any time. Or if you just need to speak to a woman, please call my wife. We are here for you."

I then asked her, "Could I please pray for you?" I was expecting an answer of something like, "Why sure," or "Oh please." Instead, Kristy raced back into my side, hugging me and weeping…again. This was one of those times that God gave me an amazing prayer for her—one of hope and healing, comfort and encouragement!

While I prayed, Kristy was holding me tight and crying. I could hear the other young nurse standing in the background, crying right along with Kristy. God is so awesome!

When I finally left, I called Leah and told her what happened. As I shared this divine encounter with her, we both cried on the phone. It was just so neat to see God's hand in this moment.

I then told her that I was on the way home. I needed to go to Walmart in Brenham and get some items. From there we could grab something to eat and then go grocery shopping at H-E-B. Afterward, we could go for one of our drives on the back roads before going home.

Okay, so far so good. No real changes on the horizon.

> The mind of man plans his way, but the Lord directs his steps. (Prov. 16:9, NASB)

Then I got home. Aha! Another small change occurred. Another redirection was taking place—unknown to me! Some book orders had come in, and I needed to get them packaged up. Leah waited for me to finish up those mailings. We left for the post office around 11:30 a.m.

We headed into the little town of Industry to go to the post office. They were getting ready to close for lunch break. I was working with the postal person when suddenly, Leah came running into the office. She was in a panic and asked to use the restroom.

"Sorry ma'am," the assistant said. "We cannot let anyone use the bathroom."

Dismayed, Leah looked at me and said, "Never mind… it is too late!" and left.

I figured that she headed off for Lindeman's Shell Station down the street to use the restroom and would be back waiting for me outside.

While I was waiting, the postal clerk locked up the post office, then handled my book mailings. When she finished, she asked me, "How much are your books?" I told her $14.00. After looking at the book for a couple of minutes, she decided that she wanted to buy the book and wrote me a check.

Yahoo! Another book sold. Praise God! I walked outside to get her a book, but the truck and Leah were both gone. So I went back inside and told her that my wife was gone with the truck. She said, "It's okay, you can bring me a copy later." I replied that I would be back later.

I walked back outside, looked around, and I finally saw the truck all the way down the street at Lindeman's Store. So off I went, down the street to the corner.

Just about the time I got to the truck, Leah was leaving the building. She looked at me and said, "Just take me home!"

She apparently did not make it in time for the bathroom, so we drove home—four miles to the house (*pee-yoo*). She was embarrassed and mad at the same time, and she was fuming!

We finally got home. She took a shower and changed and cleaned herself up. About an hour later she said, "I'm okay now. Let's go to Brenham!"

Women! They have the right to change their mind at any time!

It was about 1:00 p.m. and the post office would not open till 1:30 p.m. Since I could not deliver the book that was paid for, we kept on driving to Brenham. This would be another thirty minute drive.

Brenham, we are finally here! I thought. I pulled into the Walmart parking lot. I looked at Leah and said, "This will be quick! I will be right back." (So I thought. Ha!)

I got inside quickly, got my items really fast, checked out, and was on my way to the next stop. When suddenly, to my surprise, I looked over by the wall, and there on a park bench, lying down, was a woman from our church. I looked at her and said, "Frannie, is that you?"

A woman standing next to her was a floor manager. She looked at me and said, "Do you know this woman?"

I said, "Yes I do, she goes to my church."

Frannie, somewhat dazed and confused, looked up at me and just mumbled something. I asked her the same question again. This time she said, "Brian...Brian...Oh! Brian, is that you?"

I said, "Yes...are you okay? Are you up here by yourself?"

She said that she driven her friend May up to get groceries. I asked, "Would you like for me to go get her?"

"No...no. Let her finish shopping."

I told her that Leah was with me and that she could drive her car home if she needed to. She was emphatic. "*No. I'll be fine, and you do not need to bother Leah.*"

"Well…okay…if you are sure," I replied. Frannie was not going to let anyone help her—at least not right then.

On my way out, I gave the floor manager my card and said, "My wife just happens to be in the truck outside, and we could take her home."

She said, "Well, thank you. Are you sure it wouldn't be a problem?"

"Not at all," I replied. "In fact, we are going across the street to get a burger and then to grocery shop. So if she changes her mind, call us."

So I left the store, went outside, got in the truck, and shared the story with Leah. We had just left the parking lot when my phone rang. It was the floor manager from Walmart. She said, "Frannie has changed her mind and would like for your wife to drive her home." So we turned around and went back to the store. I dropped Leah off at the front door.

As I let Leah out, I told her, "I have got to get something to eat! You get Frannie and I will go over across the street to MacDonald's and get a burger. Call me when you are ready."

I went across the street—had to wait for the line to move so that I could park my truck. Then went inside and ordered my burger—had to make sure they cooked it well done. At last, burger in hand, I was back in my truck. As soon as I got in the truck, my phone rang: it was a call from a client.

They had some very detailed items to share with me, and they had to talk to me now. Halfway through that conversation, my phone started beeping. It was Leah on the other line. "Gotta go now!" I said. "I have a small emergency with a friend up here in Brenham. Bye!" I switched over to talk to Leah. She said they were loading up Frannie and that they would be leaving shortly.

I told her that I would be waiting on the other side of the road. I got around the corner and waited for them. I saw Frannie's car come out of the Walmart parking lot. Then suddenly it pulled over to the side of the road. *What's up now?* I thought.

I waited for a minute or two, then called Leah. "Hey! Is everything okay?" I asked.

Leah replied, "Fran was sick, I stopped to give her a minute to toss her lunch!"

After a few minutes, we were now heading to Bellville. This would be another thirty- minute drive or so, but it is only time.

First we took May home, took out her shopping bags, and then took Fran home. When we got to Frannie's house, she said, "You don't have to park my car in the garage. I will move it later." Fran got out of the car and said, "You don't have to wait with me—I am okay."

No way, I thought. I told her, "We want to stay with you 'til your sister gets here." So I went inside with her, sat with her, talked a bit with her to make sure that she was coherent and okay. Later, when her sister arrived, we prayed for her. Then Leah and I left.

Okay, you are now thinking, *Wow! Is this the end of the story?* Nope—God is not through yet!

Back in the truck, I told Leah, "We have to go back to Industry to the post office. I have to take this book back to the lady there. She has already paid for this."

We now had another thirty minutes to drive back to Industry. Once at the post office, I took the book in. Of course the postal carrier said, "You did not have to come back today. You could have dropped it off any time." I just love small towns!

I walked back outside to the truck, got in, closed the door, and just sat there. I did not say a word. I just sat there. Leah looked at me and said, "Well? Where are we going?" I didn't speak. I just sat there in silence.

Again, I heard Leah ask me a question. "Well, what are you going to do?"

I looked over at my bride and said, "I don't want to go back to Brenham! I am afraid if we head back in that direction something else is going to happen and distract us. And besides, I am not really up to a long drive home afterward."

> Lord, I know that people's lives are not their own; it
> is not for them to direct their steps. (Jer. 10:23, NIV)

"Okay, so what do you want to do?" she asked.

I told her that while I was driving behind them on the way to Frannie's home I had called my friend—let's call him Stan—who works in a small town grocery store. He wanted a book for his wife and an extra one to give away. Stan had shared with me a few weeks earlier that his wife had lost her sister, and he wanted to get a book for her. So I thought maybe we could go shop at his store in the other town. So off we went!

This day in May was one of the first days that Leah was not in her ankle boot from when she had broken her ankle. When we got to the grocery store, Leah's ankle was getting tired. She felt that she needed to find a scooter to use as her basket for shopping. We found Stan, and he found a scooter for Leah to ride in. Then he asked how much he owed us for the books. I gave him the dollar amount. He left and returned a few minutes later and paid me.

Okay, now you are thinking, *You are going to finish shopping, and we are through with the story, right?*

Think again. This is how God sets things up for a divine encounter. As the late radio talk show host Paul Harvey would say, "And now for the rest of the story!"

Stan then asked me, "Have you got a minute?" To which I replied, "Oh, sure." Meanwhile my bride, Leah drove happily off into the sunset to shop.

Stan began to share with me an update on his wife. "Brian, as you know, my wife's sister was killed in a car accident on her way to work by running into a horse.

"My wife suffered greatly with this loss. Over time my wife, in talking with me, kept saying that she wanted this woman who owned the horse to know the pain that was caused by this accident. The horse was on the road because the gate was left open accidentally."

Stan continued, "My wife was consistent and insistent on this desire. She told me over and over how she wanted this woman to know what her sister meant to her. She felt this would help her move forward in her grief. I knew how fragile my wife was from this tragedy and did everything I could to discourage her from going up to the woman's front door.

"Time passed and my wife was invited to go to a woman's Bible study at our church on the book of Ruth. She had withdrawn from the community in her grief, so this was a huge step in her going. She decided to go, and the topic this day was on loss. My wife said all kinds of emotions were coming up as the study went on, and she was just waiting for a good time to leave that would not interrupt the class. The class leader asked if anyone wanted to come to the front and speak to the class on any loss they had experienced. No one came forward, and the leader asked my wife if she would mind coming and telling the class of her recent loss of her sister. My wife was panicking inside but felt it would be terrible of her to walk out.

"She went up front and began to tell her story of the wonderful person her sister was. She shared that the wonderful relationship they had was due to the fact that they lived in the same town. She told of how sudden and tragic this loss was to her and her family and how terrible the grief was and continued to be.

"She told of how she has cried out to God, asking why this had happened. But, through it all, somehow she knew that God would see her through. As my wife finished speaking, an unknown woman came to the front, knelt, and held onto my wife's legs, crying. My wife took her face in her hands, lifted her face and asked, 'What's wrong, honey?' The woman said, 'Please forgive me. I am the woman who owned the horse that killed your sister.'"

Wow! Can you imagine this moment in time and all who witnessed this?

Stan continued, "My wife was faced with a decision: shun her, ignore her, run, or forgive. She said that the Holy Spirit came over her at that moment, and she looked the woman in her eyes as she held her face in her hands, and said, 'Of course I forgive you.' They embraced and the entire room cried. This woman had been invited by a friend of hers to the Bible study on that same day.

"How awesome is our God! He arranged for my wife to do the very thing she wanted to do without her realizing she did it until it was done. He arranged this in such a way as to minister to the woman who had been hurting the entire time as well. He also did it in a way that it ministered to many in that room that day. This was a great lesson in grief and forgiveness."

Wow! Talk about choking up and feeling the power of the Holy Spirit come through! I just stood there, stunned. And the only words that came out of my mouth were "*Praise* God!"

> And He ordered us to preach to the people, solemnly to testify that this is the One who has been appointed by God as Judge of the living and the dead. Of him, all the prophets bear witness that through Him, His name everyone who believes in Him receives forgiveness of sins. (Acts 10:42–43, NASB)

We sometimes want to say that Satan is getting in our way to distract us and detract us from our so-called appointed time and goal.

But I am reminded that Satan is the author of fear, confusion, doubt, and obstacles. It is God who redirects us and changes our path. He may do this to protect us or even to save us. Maybe, just maybe, He redirects us on our path to slow us down for an exciting divine intersection.

On this day, it was a redirection that would be used by Him for a very important purpose. Sometimes, that redirection is there just to love someone and let them know that God loves them. Sometimes it is to let someone know that He is always right there, right there by their side.

In these instances, each of us begins to understand that there is a step of faith in all things that we do.

> He who dwells in the shelter of the Most High will abide in the shadow of the Almighty. I will say to the Lord, My refuge and my fortress, My God, in whom I trust! (Ps. 91:1, NASB)

On that day in May redirection occurred several times. My schedule was altered in Katy to give comfort to a grieving young woman. Leah's and my shopping was redirected to help a fellow Christian in need. Though I was tired of driving and hungry, I trusted God to direct my steps. I didn't complain—at least, not very much. Our persistence to keep the promise of delivering a book may have a long-term purpose that I can't dream of. In the short term, God used the extra trip to the post office to redirect our steps to Stan's store, where Leah could comfortably shop while I heard a remarkable story that lifted my spirits.

That story involved redirecting a grieving woman and a guilt-ridden woman to the same Bible study on the same day where they both found release in Him.

In each of these instances, we begin to understand that there is a step of faith in all things that we do.

Learning to Release the Spirit in Your Life

Brian

> The Helper, the Holy Spirit, whom the Father will
> send in my name, will teach you everything and
> make you remember all that I have told you.
>
> —John 14:26 (GNT)

During the last couple of years that Leah and I were living in Katy, Texas, I began to really study God's Word. I don't mean that I just read a couple of passages each day or watched a little on Christian television, but I really began to seek God like I had never done before.

I picked up a *MacArthur Study Bible*, and the study notes in this Bible inspired me to read and "dig deeper" into God's Word.

Wanting even more, I began attending seminary classes at Grace UMC in Katy. They were just starting their Bible seminary, and I wanted to be part of the beginning. It was awesome learning more about basic Bible principles, and the teachers were incredible. Paul Helbeig was my mentor. Though he did not know this, he helped keep me passionate about studying the Bible. Later I had an opportunity to learn from Dr. Israel Loken. The four classes that I took over two years were informative and educational. It was an amazing time!

After Leah and I moved to the country, our Bible study time and prayer time began to increase enormously. We were doing home Bible study together and learning from some very interesting people.

We were feeling led to know more about the Holy Spirit and learning to be led by the Spirit. There would be a host of people that we would start learning from who were prompted and led by the Holy Spirit.

This group of people included Chuck Pierce, Barbie Brethitt, Fuchsia Picket, Charles and Frances Hunter (better known as Happy Hunters), and their daughter Joan. Over time, we found additional people to learn from, including the late Bob Jones and a powerful preacher named Smith Wigglesworth.

There were times that I would feel like the Lord was talking to me, and at other times I just was not sure. I would sometimes jokingly say to someone, "I feel like the Lord is speaking to me and that He is saying…"

Some of my friends would look at me and say, "Brian, do you really think the Lord is telling you that?"

With a smile on my face, I would just say, "He is either talking to me, and this is pretty far out there, or it must have been the pizza that I ate last night!" Ha!

One thing is for certain, there have been times we have had opportunities to do something and the Lord gave us permission and confirmation. With other prayers, it is has been wait, wait, and wait. For some others, the door was slammed in our faces. At those times it was like the Lord said, *stop!* And you shall go no further!

In some cases we have actually seen the Lord give us a word and tell us to postpone what we were doing. This would mean releasing others from our ministry and get back on course. He had a purpose and calling on our lives.

Those are the times that you want to look up to the sky and say, "God...*are you sure?*"

Yet there have been those really interesting times that He said, "Go ahead and I will always be with you."

So, some of you may be asking yourselves, "What does it means to release the Spirit? And will any of this help me? "

All good questions, as my friend Stephen Coffee would say.

Okay, so what does the word *release* mean?

I had to look this up in the dictionary. Here are a few meanings:

1. To set free from confinement, restraint, or bondage

2. To free from something that binds or holds back; to let go

3. To dismiss, as from a job

4. To get rid of a debt or obligation

Now here is something interesting, in Hebrew the word for *release* is *Shĕmittah* (Shi-mee-tah), and it means "to remit or release."

It also means to fling down, let rest, to shake, stumble, a remission (of debt), and suspension of labor.

This is really cool because when the Lord released us, there was a time of shaking, a suspension of the labor that went into the project and a time of rest.

> At the end of every seven years you shall grant a release. (Deut. 15:1, AMP)

With that, Leah and I wanted to share with you seven things that you need to do to release the Holy Spirit in your lives. You may agree or disagree, but for now, we are just the messengers. Enjoy and be blessed.

First, we have to "let go."

Come on, Brian, really? Let go? Yes, we have to let go, let go of the hurts.

We have to let go and become broken—to ask for forgiveness—and open ourselves up to the Lord. Basically, we must be prepared to be willing to be peeled like an onion. This means we have to forgive others, and this forgiveness includes ourselves. And we have to repent of our sins to God. This is really important.

> Create in me a clean heart, O God, and renew a right, persevering, and steadfast spirit within me. (Ps. 51:10, AMP)

> If we confess our sins, He is faithful and just to forgive
> us our sins and to cleanse us from all unrighteousness.
> (1 John 1:9, NKJV)

Second, we need to learn to forgive others.

Oh man! I do not think I can do that, Brian! Yes, you can, and here is why.

We have to learn to forgive others. If we do *not* forgive, we will harbor those ill feelings of anger and resentment, but worse than that, God will not forgive *us*!

This is a spirit of *offense*—it keeps us from being healed and being blessed.

When you take away the spirit of offense, it can open the door to true repentance and healing and remove the veil of the spirit of deceit, doubt, and hopelessness. This is true for everyone, not only for you, but for others around you.

> If you forgive others the wrongs they have done to
> you, your Father in heaven will also forgive you. But
> if you do not forgive others, then your Father will not
> forgive the wrongs you have done. (Matt. 6:14–15,
> GNB)

Third, we need to learn to release to receive.

Now this is a very powerful statement. Why? You have to learn to release everything! When you do, you gain Christ!

If we want to live a Christ-filled and joyful life, we need to learn to release *all* of the bad stuff so we can *reap* the good things and blessings in life!

> But you have an anointing from the Holy One, and you know all things. I have not written to you because you do not know the truth, but because you know it, and that no lie is of the truth. (1 Jn. 2:20–21, NKJV)

Fourth, we need to learn to Pray for His Spirit.

We need to ask the Lord for His Spirit. The Holy Spirit will guide us and tell us what is right and what is wrong.

> But the Helper, the Holy Spirit, whom the Father will send in my name, he will teach you all things and bring to your remembrance all that I have said to you. (John 14:26, ESV)

Fifth, we need to learn to yield and have obedience.

This means to stop resisting—give up and give in. Again: *let go!*

Learn to yield yourself unto the Lord. This means you have to humble yourself before the King, ask Him for guidance and direction. Learn to become open, willing, and obedient!

Just like Paul on the road to Damascus, he had a divine appointment with God. We need to have those divine appointments with God.

> And he trembling and astonished said, Lord, what wilt thou have me to do? And the Lord said unto him, Arise, and go into the city, and it shall be told thee what thou must do. (Acts 9:6, KJV)

And as soon as he, Paul, was willing to yield, he was in a condition where God could meet his need. So, as soon as we are willing to yield, to give up and give in, then God can meet our need. What an awesome God!

And when we yield, we must learn to be obedient to God. Obedience *is* sacrifice. When you are obedient, things change. Obedience brings blessings. Here is a great scripture and reminder of our obedience to God. I think this verse says it all.

> Trust God from the bottom of your heart. Don't try to figure out everything on your own. Listen for God's voice in everything you do, everywhere you go; he's the one who will keep you on track.
>
> Don't assume that you know it all. Run to God! Run from evil! Your body will glow with health; your very bones will vibrate with life!
>
> "Honor God with everything you own; give him the first and the best. But don't, dear friend, resent God's discipline;
>
> Don't sulk under His loving correction. It's the child he loves that God corrects; a father's delight is behind all this." (Prov. 3:5–12, MSG)

Sixth, we need to learn to Worship.

Yes, learn to worship the true King. Become an amazing and incredible worshipper. Worship Him in your prayers, your offerings, and your sacrifice. Really learn to worship. It is not a spectator sport.

When you do, others will see how you worship the true King and join you. Let others see how you truly worship with joy and gladness in *all things*: in your prayers, tithes, offerings, and praise!

> For the Lord is great, and greatly to be praised: he is to be feared above all gods. (Ps. 96:2, KJV)

> God is a Spirit: and they that worship him must worship him in spirit and in truth. (John 4:24, KJV)

Seventh, we need to learn *to be strong.*

Here is an interesting thing to know: In Hebrew, the word used for *strength* or *strong* is *hazak*. Now, look at the following scriptures from Joshua 1:6, 7 and 9 and look at them in a new way.

The first time *hazak* is used is in verse 6:

> Be strong and courageous, for you shall give this people possession of the land which I swore to their fathers to give them. (Josh. 1:6, NASB)

The second time the word is used is in verse 7. What God is really saying is to be *very strong*!

> Only be strong and very courageous; be careful to do according to all the law which Moses My servant commanded you; do not turn from it to the right or to the left, so that you may have success wherever you go. (Josh. 1:7, NASB)

The third time is in verse 9. God gave him a command and a definite reminder to be very, *very* strong:

> Have I not commanded you? Be strong and courageous! Do not tremble or be dismayed, for the Lord your God is with you wherever you go (Josh. 1:9, NASB).

In our journey through life, there will be different steps of faith that we will learn to walk through.

> Consider it all joy, my brethren, when you encounter various trials, knowing that the testing of your faith produces endurance. And let endurance have its perfect result, so that you may be perfect and complete, lacking in nothing. (James 1:2-4 NASB)

Part of the steps of faith is learning to release the Spirit. This is a big step in life!

So, just to recap, here are the 7 points to help you to successfully release the Spirit in your life:

1. Let go
2. Forgive others
3. Release to receive
4. Pray for His Spirit
5. Yield and have Obedience
6. Worship
7. Be Strong!

I just love the way Smith Wigglesworth spoke about God's Word:

> "Know your Book, live it, believe it, and obey it. Hide God's Word in your heart. IT will save your soul, quicken your body, illume your mind. The Word of God is full and final, infallible, reliable, and up-to-date, and our attitude toward it must be one of unquestioned obedience."

Here is one of those sharing moments, when you know that you are doing what God has called you to do.

In April 2012, my friend Lynne Wilson called me about having Leah and me come down to Holy Cross Church in Sugarland to speak with their book club. I had played keyboards with the praise team at Holy Cross Church from 2003 to 2005.

Debbie Fancher (our previous lead singer with The Daystar Project) was also there, as well as Connie Fletcher Powell and her sister Patti. Connie and I knew one another from Holy Cross as well.

Their book club had just finished reading our book and wanted to have a question and answer session with Leah and me.

There were about twelve ladies who came this evening. It was a great group; we ended up being there for over two hours!

The group asked some really great questions about the book, our story, how we reacted and responded during the first days. They also shared that a number of them had bought books and also bought e-books for their Kindles.

A couple of the ladies asked some very deep and thought-provoking questions. Leah and I, with God's help, answered all of them. Many were very thankful for the way that we were transparent and shared our innermost thoughts.

Some of the ladies shared that they had been using some of the stories from our book to lift up them up and encourage them in their walk.

They asked about our ministry. They were really excited when we told them about our name and how we got the name of Hazak—it means strength and encouragement.

One of the ladies used a phrase that we hear over and over again when we speak. She said, "You do know that people are watching you, don't you?" She went on to say that she could see the God's light in our faces and in our speech. His anointing was on us! It was very apparent.

One of the ladies shared that they had lost their son two years ago on March 14. She came up to me later and wanted to know if her husband could call me and speak with me. Wow! What an honor!

A couple of other ladies had lost children. One young lady lost her dad when she was only ten years old. I asked her if her mom had remarried. Her response stunned me. She said, "Yes—several times."

Wow! How sad—several marriages. The loss must have been very hard on her mom, as well as for her.

A number of the ladies who came up afterward to get their books signed were also very thankful for the way that we responded to the crisis in the book.

One question asked was, "How did you manage to hold things together in lieu of the fact that many couples end their marriages after the loss of a child?"

We told them that it was about coming together and making a determination to stay together. That we both had to get on our knees and ask for help and pray for supernatural peace. It is that peace that goes beyond all understanding.

> And the peace of God, which transcends all understanding, will guard your hearts and your minds in Christ Jesus (Phil. 4:7, NIV).

I am reminded that a man is never taller than when he is on his knees before God.

We then talked about our "drives" and how important they were—and how we first got started on the drives.

Lynne Wilson shared about knowing me and being around me and the fact that my "Type A" personality and control of life was a driving force for me. But she also said that I was humble in the way that God worked through me. This came across to others in the church and praise team.

Debbie Fancher shared that when she met us that there was something different about us—that we were very positive and loving and outgoing. When she found out about Victoria, she was stunned and in awe of how we were—that God really flowed throughout our lives in every way. Wow! What an awesome God we serve!

Leah was given a very nice vase with two pink/red roses. On the way home she read to me a card that we both received. It was a wonderful card that stated:

> God is using YOU—for His special purpose
>
> To SHINE His light
>
> To Share His love
>
> To Shape His people

WOW! All that we could say was **WOW!**

Inside of the card there was folded up piece of pink tissue. Inside the tissue was a wonderful love offering.

Leah shared that this was another confirmation from God that we were on the right track—that this is just the beginning.

We talked about how we loved to speak to groups. It was fun and exciting that we could really encourage people. This is our hearts' desire to serve Him!

I had shared earlier the scripture verse from John 14:26 from the Good News Bible. I want to close out this chapter with the same scripture passage, but this is from The Message Bible. I think it rocks!

> I'm telling you these things while I'm still living with you. The Friend, the Holy Spirit whom the Father will send at my request, will make everything plain to you.

> He will remind you of all the things I have told you.
> I'm leaving you well and whole. That's my parting gift
> to you. Peace. I don't leave you the way you're used
> to being left—feeling abandoned, bereft. So don't be
> upset. Don't be distraught. (John 14:26, MSG)

So, just think, if Jesus did this for the disciples, don't you think He can make everything plain to us? Jesus told us that He would send the Holy Spirit to help us.

That is His promise. I guarantee it!

Bible Scripture References

Amplified Version (AMP)
English Standard Version (ESV)
Good News Translation (GNT)
King James Version (KJV)
New American Standard Bible (NASB)
New International Version (NIV)
New King James Version (NKJV)
New Living Translation (NLT)
The Living Bible (TLB)
The Message (MSG)
World English Bible (WEB)

CPSIA information can be obtained at www.ICGtesting.com
Printed in the USA
LVOW07s0548300716

498224LV00007B/11/P